Jeremiah:
The Prophet Who Wouldn't Quit

WILLIAM J. PETERSEN

Recommended Dewey Decimal Classification: 224.2
Suggested Subject Heading: BIBLE O.T.—BIOGRAPHY

Library of Congress Catalog Card Number: 83-51307
ISBN: 978-1-60126-097-0

Printed by
Masthof Press
219 Mill Road
Morgantown, PA 19543-9516
www.masthof.com

Contents

About the Author

William J. Petersen has written more than 30 books and hundreds of magazine articles.

After serving as a newspaper editor in the Midwest, he was named editorial director of *Christian Life Magazine* and *Christian Bookseller Magazine*. Moving east, he became editorial director and later editor of *Eternity Magazine* in Philadelphia.

He is a past-president of the Evangelical Press Association and became the first recipient of the Joseph T. Bayly award given by the Evangelical Press Association for "Oustanding Service in Christian Periodical Publishing." Eastern College (now Eastern University) has awarded him an honorary doctorate for his leadership in Christian journalism.

In 1986 he moved into book publishing and became editorial director and later vice president of Fleming H. Revell Publishing.

More than a million copies of his books have been sold and have been translated into more than 20 languages. In his retirement, he has been writing a series of detective spoofs called The Octogenarian Sleuth, set in his current residence, The Palisades of Broadmoor Park, Colorado Springs.

To Kathy,
For empathy with sparkle

Introduction

I didn't always like Jeremiah.

A crybaby, a complainer, perhaps a bit neurotic. That was the notion I used to have of him. Besides, he wrote one of the longest books in the Bible. (When I was growing up, I had a decided preference for Old Testament books like Obadiah and New Testament books like Jude.)

But at that time I really didn't know Jeremiah. All my knowledge about him was secondhand. Even when I read a few verses from his book, I never stayed with him long enough to get to know him well. From my fleeting acquaintance with him, he seemed to live in another world, long ago and far away.

Then for some reason I began to read his book in depth and take a hard look at the man.

What a man! And what a story!

Since then, I have realized how frequently I find myself in "Jeremiah-like" spots, and I respond by going to the Bible and seeing how Jeremiah responded.

Let me define a "Jeremiah-like" spot. It's when you're squeezed in the middle. You may be a go-between and find yourself misunderstood. You may be given a job you really don't want to do, because it's a no-win situation. You may be frustrated in doing God's will; nothing of eternal value seems to be happening. In the middle of all this, you may find yourself questioning a God who seems a bit removed from you right now. At present, God's call to you may seem in the distant past. The present seems as if you're hitting your head against a brick wall. The future, more of the same. Well, you say, that's my situation, all right. But why do I need to read about someone with the same problems? Because in Jeremiah we find some answers. As we grapple with the problems that confronted Jeremiah, we can wrestle more effectively with the problems in our own lives.

Now admittedly, Jeremiah isn't a simple man, and his book isn't a simple book either. The organization of his book has baffled scholars, but basically the first 25 chapters contain an anthology of sermons interspersed with some "off-the-record" asides that Jeremiah poignantly utters to God. To further complicate matters, the sermons are not in any particular order. Then from chapters 26—45, you have a sketchy biography of Jeremiah; but this is not really in chronological order either. Finally, in the last section of his book, chapters 46—52, you find prophecies against other nations.

George Adam Smith likened the Book of Jeremiah to the works of other Eastern poets which "are like canoe voyages in Canada, in which the canoe now glides down a stream and is again carried overland by what are called portages to other streams or other branches of the same stream."

But it really isn't as hopeless as it may seem. Despite the rather jumbled nature of his book, we know more about Jeremiah's life than we know of the life of any other prophet, with the possible exception of Daniel. With Daniel, however, you only know the outside; with Jeremiah, you know and feel the inside of the man. Unlike Daniel, you don't find Jeremiah in a lions' den. You find him in a slimy cistern, oozing in deeper and deeper all the time. I can identify with that.

Unlike Daniel, you don't find Jeremiah interpreting dreams for the king and being rewarded with honor and prestige. You find him under house arrest, dictating a lengthy manuscript to a disgruntled secretary; then after the manuscript is read in the king's chamber, the monarch gets out his penknife, cuts up the manuscript page by page, and throws Jeremiah's masterpiece into the fire. If you have ever felt that you were under house arrest and couldn't get the message out, you will be able to identify with Jeremiah.

Unlike Daniel, Jeremiah doesn't see his prayers answered immediately; unlike Daniel, Jeremiah wrestles with doubts; unlike Daniel, Jeremiah receives no promotions, gains no regal commendations, gets invited to no royal festivities. Maybe you can identify with those things too.

Basically, Jeremiah is very human. Maybe that's why I have come to enjoy Jeremiah. Yes, I said *enjoy*.

It seems wrong—almost sinful—to ask anyone to enjoy Jeremiah. Through much of the book you will be weeping with him, and seldom will you be able to laugh with him. But by the time you finish, you will have experienced a strange kind of enjoyment through getting to know a very human prophet.

1

Getting a Job You Don't Want

Jeremiah 1:1-8

I'm not cut out for this, Lord.

What are you cut out for?

I'm cut out for—well, I'm cut out to do the things I want to do.

And that doesn't include cleaning the toilet bowls and taking out the garbage. Right?

Right. But I don't mean that kind of thing. I mean, I'm not cut out to do things that are contrary to my psychological makeup.

Do you know your psyche better than I do?

Well, Lord, let me put it another way. You've given me certain spiritual gifts—at least that's what my pastor has been telling me—First Corinthians, I think it is.

That's right. I have.

But why do I end up being called on to do things that aren't in line with what I think my spiritual gifts are? It's not that I don't want to do what You want me to do, Lord: it's that the gifts and abilities You've given me don't always match the job You've assigned to me. I'm sure there are other people better suited for the job than I am. Why don't You get them to do the job? Why me, Lord—why me?

* * * * * *

If that's the way you sometimes feel, join the club.
That's the way it was for Jeremiah too.

God had no business asking Jeremiah to do those nasty assignments; certainly God could have found others who were more psychologically suited for the job than Jeremiah.

To put it bluntly, Jeremiah appeared to be miscast. He just wasn't cut out for what God was asking him to do.

Maybe you feel that God has miscast you as well.

You're the silent type and He has asked you to witness.

You're a Martha and He has asked you to be a Mary.

You're a noncombatant and He wants you to get involved in the thick of things.

Jeremiah was a poet, and God was calling him to be a prophet. He could have been a sensitive balladeer, writing folksongs for all Judah to sing. God, however, called him to a ministry of thunder and lightning instead of a ministry of gentle spring rains.

One commentator describes Jeremiah as "shy and sensitive, honest and human, somewhat impatient and impulsive, given to times of elation and dejection, courageous and confident, yet torn by a sense of inadequacy and an inner conflict between natural inclination and a sense of divine vocation."

F.B. Meyer diagnoses Jeremiah as a man "conscious of his helplessness, yearning for sympathy and love he was never to know." A poet, not a prophet.

"Torn by a sense of inadequacy. . . yearning for a sympathy and love he was never to know." You know people like that?

Getting to Know Jeremiah

Born about 646 B.C. (give or take five years), Jeremiah was reared in the suburban town of Anathoth, three hilly miles northeast of Jerusalem. It was about an hour's walk, but as a teenager Jeremiah no doubt ran the distance in half that time.

Anathoth was a hotbed of gossip. News of all kinds swirled like the dust blown by the hot sirocco winds on the dry dirt lanes of the little village.

Priests and Levites had been commuting between Solomon's temple and Anathoth for years. Anathoth had been a community of priests and Levites since Joshua's time (Josh. 21:18); its most famous resident had been Abiathar, the priest who counselled King David for many years (1 Sam. 22:20-23). In Jeremiah's day, there were more priests than jobs in the temple. In fact, Phoenician and Assyrian deities were worshiped in the temple more often than Jehovah, and the king had appointed special priests to make sure that the foreign deities got equal time. Some of the local priests set up a shrine in Anathoth. It seemed to bring religion closer to the people, and various gods were worshiped there, including, of course, Jehovah.

Jeremiah's father, Hilkiah, was a priest. But whether he was active or inactive, whether he served in Jerusalem or Anathoth, it is difficult to determine. Most scholars doubt that Hilkiah was an active priest or Jeremiah probably would have mentioned it. Theoretically, Hilkiah and his family were supposed to have been supported by the tithes of Jewish temple worshipers. But considering the apathy of the people, Hilkiah probably brought home more rumors and gossip than food for the family table.

In addition to knowing all the latest gossip from Jerusalem, Anathothians were well aware of any rumblings up north. Judah's northern frontier lay only three or four miles beyond Anathoth and that was a bit too close for comfort. Whenever Judah was in jeopardy, the odds were that the trouble would be coming from the north. Of course, with Egypt to the south, Edom to the east, and Phoenicia to the west, you couldn't exactly say that Jeremiah's native land was surrounded by friends.

So maybe you can imagine what Jeremiah was hearing and seeing as he grew up. Crime in the streets of Jerusalem . . . homosexuals roaming the temple . . . corruption in the palace . . . infants offered on pagan altars between Anathoth and Jerusalem . . . war clouds in the north, threats from the west, raids from the east, and a general feeling that things were going downhill. That was Jeremiah's environment.

With one ear, Jeremiah could hear the sordid gossip seeping out of Jerusalem and with the other, he could hear the rumbles of trouble in the north. And all around him were priests, many of whom were disgruntled and unemployed, while others were discouraged, prone to compromise with open idolatry in the temple and merely going through the motions of religious service. More and more of the local priests were sympathetic to the local shrine.

When Jeremiah was born, Manasseh was the king. It would be hard to imagine a more horrendous monarch than he. His reign was bloody, vile, and filthily pagan. He could go down in the history books along with Nero, Attila the Hun, and Hitler.

Jeremiah was still a lad when Manasseh died and his son Amon took the throne. Amon showed promise of being a carbon copy of his father, but unnamed assassins eliminated him two years after his inauguration.

That opened the door for Josiah, Amon's 8-year-old son, who became king in 639 b.c. For the folks in Anathoth, the child-king must have been a ray of hope, though admittedly only a ray. Godly people—and there were still a few of them around—were sick and tired of the corruption of the previous two regimes.

But the two big questions were: (1) Why should Josiah be any different from his father and grandfather, and (2) Even if he were, how could a little boy—8 years old—make a difference?

Jeremiah must have heard these questions too, and as a lad only a year or two younger than Josiah, he must have hoped that God could use boys as well as men.

God could. Eight years later, when Josiah was 16 (about 631 b.c.), he "began to seek after the God of David" (2 Chron. 34:3, kjv). That's when things started to happen.

History records that Assyria's powerful king died shortly thereafter, and that paved the way for the teenage king to assert his political, as well as religious, independence. Four years later (about 627 B.C.), Josiah decided that if Jehovah was good enough for him, Jehovah was good enough for his people. He began to throw out the Assyrian and Palestinian gods that dotted the Judean landscape and had degraded his nation's culture.

None of this was done overnight; the pagan religion had become too deeply ingrained for that. But the movement was in the right direction.

It was enough to make a teenager like Jeremiah find a lute or a sackbut and write some doxologies. But while Jeremiah was still shopping for a lute, something else happened.

"I Knew Him When...."

The year was now 626 B.C. Jeremiah was probably close to 20 years old and well into a year he would never forget, for this was the year that God so boldly intruded into his life, and called him to an impossible mission.

That is the scene when the curtain opens on the first chapter of Jeremiah's book. There you see young Jeremiah all alone on a naked stage with the spotlight on him. Behind the scenes, the stagehands are bustling around. In the wings, other actors are waiting for their cues. But for now, the spotlight is on Jeremiah.

The interchange was one-to-one, God and Jeremiah. A mere mortal is at a decided disadvantage in such a situation.

You remember when God put His magnificent spotlight on Saul of Tarsus, that angry young man hurrying to Damascus? Others were with him, but his confrontation with God was one-to-one (Acts 9:1-6).

Remember Zaccheus up in a tree? "Come down, Zaccheus," said the Master, shining His spotlight on him. And a diminutive tax collector came to the audit that was done one-on-one (Luke 19:1-6).

God is not stereotyped in His dealings with us. He comes in various ways and with differing techniques. You may be traveling down a road like Saul, up a tree like Zaccheus, or growing up like Jeremiah. God calls men and women of all ages and from all vocations. He seems to enjoy variety in disciples as He does in snowflakes.

But whenever and however the Divine Intruder comes to you, He will get your attention, just as assuredly as He got Jeremiah's.

It was not necessary to use a lightning bolt on Jeremiah. Nor was there a choir of angels. (Perhaps a little later on, Jeremiah would have welcomed a little music in the background.) Jeremiah was already on speaking terms with Jehovah and so the dramatics weren't needed.

Sometimes those who are reared in Christian homes have conversion experiences which seem very ordinary. And yet what God said to Jeremiah was not ordinary at all.

If a high school classmate becomes famous, we sometimes brag, "I knew him when. . . ." But what grabbed Jeremiah's attention was that the Almighty God was telling him, "I knew you when"—and Jeremiah was anything but famous.

God told Jeremiah that he was known even before his conception. In fact, before Jeremiah was born, God had given him a job to do. That is guaranteed employment. Samson (Jud. 13:3-5), John the Baptist (Luke 1:15), and Paul (Gal.1:15-16) were also preordained for their work. The Psalmist David marvelled that God knew him while he was still in his mother's womb and while his bones were still taking shape (Ps. 139:13).

That is true of you as well.

God is always "previous." He is always a step ahead of you. This is a very comforting thought when you are about to turn a dark corner in your life. And no matter how early you wake up for breakfast, He is always at the table ahead of you.

"I Don't Want This Job!"

Do you remember how you used to choose up teams when you were a youngster? Two captains were appointed, and then the captains chose the players they wanted one by one. You hoped you would be one of the early ones selected. You certainly didn't want to be the last one standing there, finally picked by a captain mumbling under his breath, "Do I *have* to take *him?*"

I remember once choosing players for my team who weren't even there yet. "If Joe comes, he's on my side." I wanted Joe so much that I selected him, knowing that I might have to play with only eight players for an inning or two before he showed up. It was still a bit of a risk because even though Joe had promised to come, he wasn't there yet, and his mother may have detained him to mow the lawn or dry the dishes.

God had said, "When Jeremiah comes, he's on My side." And there was no risk about it. God knew that Jeremiah would come. And Jeremiah wanted to play on God's team; no doubt about it. But Jeremiah didn't want to play the position that God had asked him to play.

When I was growing up, we always had nine boys wanting to pitch and none wanting to catch. Some even claimed that their mothers didn't allow them to catch. But our real reason was that the catcher got hit with foul tips and occasionally by an errant bat. His teammates yelled at him when he couldn't grab a wild pitch or when he threw the ball on two bounces to the shortstop whenever someone was trying to steal second.

That was the problem. God had asked Jeremiah to be the catcher: to get hit with foul tips and flung bats, to be yelled at and ridiculed. Nobody likes that.

It's nice to be chosen, and perhaps nicer to be *pre*-chosen. Yet sometimes you have your own idea about what position you are best suited to play. Thus we thank God for choosing us, but we complain about our specific tasks.

Solomon wrote, "The Lord has made everything for His own purpose" (Prov. 16:4, TLB). In modern parlance, "God has a wonderful plan for your life." As Jeremiah read the fine print, however, he didn't think the day by day details of that plan were so wonderful.

Making Excuses to God

Two reactions probably chased each other through Jeremiah's mind. The first reaction was, "Who, me?" He must have felt that he was opening someone else's mail. The Divine Postman must have stuffed the wrong letter into his box.

But on the heels of that reaction came another, as he thought about the nature of the assignment. "A prophet to the nations? That would be like yelling 'Halt' to a stampede of buffalo. Those nations aren't in a mood to listen—and even if they were, they wouldn't be able to put the brakes on fast enough to avoid trampling you into the dust."

Jeremiah must have felt as if he had been appointed a goodwill ambassador to Cuba. His first words of response came out, "Ah, Sovereign Lord, I do not know how to speak; I am only a child" (Jer. 1:6).

Jeremiah was just as illogical as we sometimes are in talking back to God. His mistake was in admitting that the Lord was sovereign.

When you own God as sovereign, the "I-don't-know-hows" and the "onlys" don't matter. The Sovereign has power, supreme power in His realm.

Apparently, Jeremiah didn't realize that when God appoints, His appointments are always accompanied by His presence and His power.

Excuses seem to come naturally when we deal with God. By this time you can be sure that He has heard them all. Moses said he couldn't talk, and no one would listen to him when he did (Ex. 4:1, 10). At least, that was his excuse. Gideon thought he was too insignificant for God to use; besides that, he wasn't sure whether or not the angel wasn't his cousin Jethro or someone else playing a trick on him (Jud. 6:15, 17). Isaiah, on the other hand, thought he was too sinful to serve the Holy God (Isa. 6:5).

Jeremiah thought he was too young. Who would listen to a fuzzy-cheeked kid talking about doom and damnation? Even though he was about 20, he would still have been considered a child according to the Hebrew customs.

But, as the Apostle Paul pointed out to the Corinthians, God's choices are often unlikely. When He chooses His ball team, He doesn't select the biggest, the roughest, and the toughest. And He explains why too. "So that no one may boast before Him" (1 Cor. 1:29). God bypasses the number one draft choices and selects a team of Jeremiahs. That's how you and I got on the squad. God didn't deny that Jeremiah was young. For that matter, He didn't deny that Moses couldn't speak, that Gideon was insignificant, or that Isaiah was sinful. But any excuse is beside the point; when God sends you on an errand, excuses are irrelevant.

What God told Jeremiah could well be paraphrased in the hymn, "How Firm a Foundation":

Fear not, I am with thee, O be not dismayed,
For I am thy God and will still give thee aid;
I'll strengthen thee, help thee, and cause thee to stand,
Upheld by My gracious, omnipotent hand.
When through fiery trials thy pathway shall lie,
My grace, all sufficient, shall be thy supply;
The flames shall not hurt thee, I only design
Thy dross to consume, and thy gold to refine.

Be Honest

We can draw a few helpful conclusions from Jeremiah's initial round with the Almighty:

1. It is not wrong to admit your own inadequacy to the Lord. In fact, it is wholesome. It was the lesson that the Apostle Paul learned. God told him, "My grace is sufficient for you, for My power is perfected in weakness." Paul concluded, "Therefore I am well content with weaknesses, with insults, with distresses, with persecutions, with difficulties, for Christ's sake; for when I am weak, then I am strong" (2 Cor. 12:9-10, NASB).

2. It is not wrong to be honest with God about your feelings. Be open with the Lord about them, but make sure you allow the Lord to have the last word. We often want to understand God's entire game plan; we want to visualize the last act of the play as the curtain opens on the first. But the Lord does not reveal everything at once. Thus, His last word may be simply, "Trust Me for what you cannot see."

3. Take God's "Fear not" into battle with you. Jeremiah was just one of a long line of biblical characters whom God told not to be afraid. (Abraham, Moses, Daniel, Mary, Peter, and Paul, for example.) Fear is natural, but it also can be debilitating. It is not because God eliminates opposition or removes us from problems, that we do not need to fear. It is because He will be with us (Isa. 41:10).

God's presence does not mean that every game will be won or that every venture will be successful. There will be defeats. In fact, the defeats may outnumber the victories. But if God has called you, even as He called Jeremiah, and if His presence is with you, even as it was with Jeremiah, the outcome of each skirmish can be left in His hands.

Trust Him, even when you feel you are playing out of position.

2

Jeremiah's Secret Pitch

Jeremiah 1:9-19

My second grade teacher asked us what we wanted to be when we grew up. I think all second grade teachers do that. In our class about 12 of the girls wanted to become nurses and 3 wanted to become teachers.

Among the boys, 10 aspired to be cowboys, 3 hoped to become firemen, and 2 of us wanted to become professional baseball players.

I was one of the two.

My aspiration lasted until I was in junior high, when I failed to make the school team. That just about ended the dream. I realized that the only way I could ever possibly become a professional ball player was if I somehow developed a secret pitch, a dipsy doodle, that no batter could ever hit. I practiced with a Ping-Pong ball with some success. With a baseball, I had no success whatever.

Bruce Sutter, on the other hand, was a man who developed a secret pitch, and he has become one of the premier relief pitchers in baseball.

Of course, Bruce Sutter had enough natural ability to make it to the major leagues, but he realized that he was certainly not good enough to become a star. In fact, he probably wouldn't have lasted more than two or three years. He was what they call a marginal player.

Then one year, someone showed him how to throw a "split-fingered fastball," a pitch which no one else had ever perfected.

Bruce Sutter perfected it. As the batter sees it, the ball looks like a normal fastball. Then when it gets about five feet from the plate, it drops precipitously; the batter, of course, swings foolishly.

As a pitcher, Bruce Sutter lives and dies by his split-fingered fastball. If he didn't have it, he would have to drop out of baseball. Without it, he is nothing.

I think of Jeremiah as a seventh-century B.C. version of Bruce Sutter. Both Jeremiah and Sutter knew how far their own abilities would take them. For Sutter, it would be back to the minor leagues. For Jeremiah, it would be back to the sandlots of Anathoth. But each of them were given a secret pitch, and that made all the difference.

Bruce Sutter, of course, learned how to throw a split-fingered fastball. But what was Jeremiah given?

A Live Weapon

Jeremiah had hardly finished making his excuses to God—that he was too young and that he couldn't speak—when God touched his mouth (Jer. 1:9).

That action did not make Jeremiah a silver-tongued orator, but when God said, "I have put My words in your mouth," Jeremiah had a future.

Now let me use a baseball analogy again.

One pitcher can throw a ball just as fast as another pitcher, but one pitcher is successful, and the other is not. In baseball, they speak of successful fastball pitchers who throw "live" fastballs. A "live" fastball is a pitch that *does* something; it is active. It may move upward; it may move downward. But you can always be sure that it is going to do something.

That's what we mean when we speak of God's Word as being alive. It *does* things.

The writer of the Epistle to the Hebrews spoke of it as alive and powerful (Heb. 4:12). It is not a person; it is certainly not the fourth person of the Trinity, but still it has a certain kind of life.

In Genesis 2, God breathed into man the breath of life and he became a living soul (2:7). In 2 Timothy 3, the Scriptures are described as God-breathed or as we translate it "inspired," and thus they too have a form of God's life in them (3:16).

William Barclay in *New Testament Words* (Westminster Press, 1974) writes, "In Jewish thought a word was more than a sound expressing a meaning; a word actually did things. The Word of God is not simply a sound; it is an effective cause. God said, ' "Let there be light," and there was light' (Gen. 1:3). 'By the word of the Lord the heavens were made . . . for He spake and it was done' (Ps. 33:6, 9). He sent His Word and healed them (Ps. 107:20). God's Word will accomplish that which God pleases (Isa. 55:11). Always we must remember that in Jewish thought God's Word not only said things, it did things." Like Bruce Sutter's split-fingered fastball.

The phrase, "the Word of the Lord" keeps popping up throughout Jeremiah's prophecy. In fact, out of 97 times that the phrase appears in the Old Testament, 49 times it occurs in Jeremiah, almost once in every chapter.

When Jeremiah says—as he does frequently—"The Word of the Lord came to me," translators struggle to convey the force of the meaning. One translates it, "The Word of the Lord became an active reality with me." Another refers to a word-event happening to Jeremiah. God's Word made things happen; in fact, it was a happening in itself.

I don't know if you have ever had God's Word grip you and possess you in the same way. As you read through the prophecy of Jeremiah, you find that the prophet himself had a hard time expressing what was taking place. God's Word had an almost indescribable power.

The Word pressed in on him. In one place he says the Word burned inside him like fire in his bones (Jer. 20:9). No way could he contain it; sooner or later the fire would burn out of control.

He speaks of eating God's Word (15:16). At times it caused him joy; sometimes it caused him to stagger like a drunken man (23:9); sometimes it caused him pain (38:6, 9).

Sometimes God's Word came to Jeremiah after meditation and prayer, but it was not something that he controlled. It was something that controlled him. Often it went against his wishes, and when it did, that hurt him more.

From the start, Jeremiah knew that it was God's Word, not his. And yet he was more than an errand boy for God. He became the embodiment of the Word. Jeremiah also knew that God would accomplish His Word as He willed. Once the Word was spoken by Jeremiah, it seemed to have a life of its own. It did things.

God's opening commission to Jeremiah was, "I have set you this day over nations and over kingdoms, to pluck up and to break down, to destroy and to overthrow, to build and to plant" (1:10, RSV).

If you look at that verse alone, you might think that Jeremiah was going to do all these things by himself. But the previous verse explains how: "I have put My words in your mouth."

I doubt if Jeremiah liked the percentages in his commission: "Pluck up, break down, destroy, and overthrow" were all negative and destructive. Of the six verbs used, only one third were positive. Jeremiah probably wished that it might be at least 50-50. But that was not the task to which God had appointed him.

For Jeremiah, the Word was to have a negative mission. True, Jeremiah could liken God's Word to wheat which gives life, but more often it was like a hammer which breaks apart the seemingly indestructible.

Sometimes we think of the Word of God given unto the prophets as revealing history. Jeremiah knew that the Word was much more than a revealer of history. It actually made history happen.

But there is no reason to think of it as powerful in the past tense. It is powerful in the present tense as well. Repeatedly we are told that the Word of God endures forever. That means that its attributes are enduring as well.

Whether Jeremiah knew what a powerful secret weapon he had, I don't know. At any rate, God had to shake Jeremiah a bit to make him realize what was really going on.

The Watcher

In the mid-1960s the "God is dead" movement was in vogue among certain modern theologians. In Jeremiah's day, the prevalent philosophy seemed to be "God is asleep."

After all, how many miracles had Jehovah performed in the last couple of generations? Did God really care what was going on? His people were under the thumb of Assyria or Egypt even though they talked about their national independence. Did God care? Now morality was declining rapidly; Kings Manasseh and Amon had encouraged apostasy, and the boy-king Josiah was too new on the job to make his influence felt.

Of course, Jeremiah knew that God wasn't asleep, but he too needed a reminder.

God gave him a reminder by means of a vision. This doesn't mean that Jeremiah went into a trance. More likely he was walking along a lane in Anathoth some late winter day in 626 B.C. Possibly he was meditating on the divine call that God had given him not too many weeks before.

As he looked around him, everything seemed dark, dismal, and very dead. Spiritually, everything seemed dark, dismal, and very dead too. When would God do something?

And then Jeremiah noticed a tree along the lane. It was an almond tree, and his attention was particularly drawn to a flowering branch (1:11). In Hebrew the word for almond branch is *saqed*, which literally means "the waker." It was given that name because the almond tree was the first to bloom in the spring. Like the crocus, the peach tree, and the robin, it was a sign that spring was just around the corner. The amazing thing about the almond tree is that it flowers even before its leaves unfold.

The almond tree could be called God's wake-up call to nature.

It wasn't hard to make an application. God was awake, watching over His people and soon a spiritual spring would come (v. 12). The word for watching over is also very similar to the word for almond tree.

The expression could be used of a night watchman in the last watch of the night. He was awake and watching; morning would soon come.

Once again the emphasis was on God's Word. God had put His words in Jeremiah's mouth; now He was guaranteeing Jeremiah that these words would be fulfilled. He would watch over His Word to do it. One commentator aptly put it: "God is not emeritus. This is still His world, and He is very much awake and at work in it."

When we read the sordid headlines in the newspapers and when we go about the mundane details of day-to-day living, we sometimes overlook the fact that God is still awake and watching over His Word. And not only is He watching over His Word; He is also watching over His children.

God is awake; we are the ones who are sleeping.

Trouble's Coming

Perhaps it was the same day that Jeremiah noticed a wide-mouthed cooking pot, no doubt resting on rocks on three sides (v. 13). The fourth side was open so that wood could be placed under the pot and a fire started. As I say, there was nothing unusual about that. It was a common sight in every Hebrew home.

But what was unusual was that the rocks were of different heights, so the pot wasn't level. Besides that, the liquid in the pot was boiling, and it seemed that as it seethed, it would soon spill its contents in the direction it was leaning.

Again, God asked Jeremiah to describe the situation. Jeremiah said that he saw the pot tipping from the north toward the south. The scalding liquid would soon boil over onto the southern part of the room.

God made the obvious interpretation for Jeremiah. Trouble was coming from the north and Judah in the south would soon

be scalded (vv. 14-16). The enemy was not specifically identified, but at least Jeremiah now had a message to deliver that
would grab the attention of his listeners.

Trouble in the north was not good news, but God was in
control. He would not be taken by surprise.

Yet God indicated to Jeremiah that His Word needed
something. It needed legs. To be specific, Jeremiah's legs.

God is certainly at work in the world, but He wants us to
work side by side with Him. The promise to Jeremiah (vv. 17-
19) is similar to the promise to Joshua ("Be strong and of good
courage") and to the Ephesians ("Put on the whole armor of
God").

"Mr. Word of God"

God didn't sugarcoat Jeremiah's future. Jeremiah was in for a
battle. His whole world would erupt against him. The Babylonians would terrorize Judah, and Judah would terrorize Jeremiah.

It certainly doesn't sound like a good spot to be in, does it?
But, God told Jeremiah, you will stand impregnable. Why?
Because I am with you and I am impregnable. "I am with you
to deliver you" (v. 19, RSV). If it weren't for God's presence, it
would be difficult indeed to face the struggles of life. But with
His presence and with the awareness that He is watching over
you and that He cares for you, it makes all the difference in the
world.

Jeremiah needed God's assurance. As God's prophet, he
was not only an errand boy, he was also the embodiment of
the message. In a sense, he would be the message incarnate.

For some reason, in those days, it was thought that if you
could capture the prophet, you could curtail his message.
Certainly Jezebel had thought so. She had imagined that if she
could kill Elijah, all her problems would be over (1 Kings
19:2). But God had watched over Elijah, even as He now
would be watching over Jeremiah.

Like his predecessor Elijah, Jeremiah became "Mr. Word of
God" to the people. Of course, that didn't win him any

popularity contests; even the hometown folks in Anathoth didn't point with proverbial pride at their small-town boy making good. In fact, in their eyes, he was a disgrace. He was a blot against their community.

Why upset the apple cart, Jeremiah?

Why?

Because he had been possessed by the Word of God.

In 1521, Martin Luther was summoned before the Diet of Worms. Standing before the secular and ecclesiastical rulers of Europe, Luther was asked to retract his writing which had been condemned as heretical. In his famous reply, the Reformer answered, "I am bound by the Scriptures I have quoted, and my conscience is captive to the Word of God. I cannot and will not retract anything."

Jeremiah too was captive to the Word of God. He could not and would not retract anything either.

Let the Word Get to You

How does one become captive to the Word of God? What is involved?

You have to get into the Word; that is true, but it's even more important that the Word get into you. It must be applied and lived. It must be massaged into your soul by the Holy Spirit.

Several years ago in an African newspaper called *African Challenge*, an article entitled "Rules for Bible Study" by A.T. de B. Wilmot appeared.

The 10 rules are worth repeating:

1. Read the Bible itself. Commentaries are helpful. Devotional guides are practical, but no book is a substitute for the Bible itself.

2. Read it with prayer. It is God's Book. Jeremiah was related both to God's revelation—His Word—and to the Holy Spirit. So must we be.

3. Read a different part of the Bible every day. Don't try to read too much, but read enough so that you understand the context. God gives no badges for reading 10 chapters a day.

4. Read your Bible with your full attention and concentration. The best time for someone else may not be the best time for you. But whenever your time for Bible study comes, make the most of it.

5. Believe what you read in the Bible and admit its truth. Your mind-set is important. Like the Israelites of old, we should say "Amen" to the Word of God, even to the parts we don't like.

6. Read the Bible without prejudice and with an open mind. Don't force your preconceived notions onto God's Word. Don't try to find support for your pet theories. Let God speak to you through His Word. You've probably been involved in conversations with people who only hear what they want to hear. Sometimes we come to the Bible like that.

7. Put what you read in the Bible into your heart, personality, and character. In the New Testament, James talked about a man who looked at himself in the mirror, saw something was wrong, but walked away forgetting all about it (James 1:23-24). Jeremiah wasn't like that. Nor should we be.

8. Memorize what you read in the Bible and make it part of your character. If you can't memorize a whole verse, memorize just a portion of it, but the important thing is to assimilate what you have memorized into your lifestyle. If you take a verse with you all day long, it will help you do that.

9. Let the Word of God control all parts of your life. God's Word should control your eyes, ears, mouth, hands, feet, and brain. The Bible is not peripheral: it is not an add-on. It is to be an integral part of your thinking and acting mechanism. It is to be at the control center of your being.

10. Be prepared to make sacrifices. Sometimes we enter the Christian life to escape problems. But if you are serious about having God's Word control your being, you must be willing to live on God's terms, not your own. As long as things go well and life is rosy, it is easy to allow the Word of God to dominate your life. But when living for God entails sacrifice, we want to take the controls back in our own hands.

Jeremiah must have been tempted to do that. I'm sure that

he didn't enjoy the sacrifices he was called upon to make. Yet in spite of the fact that he frequently complained to God about his lot in life, he left the controls in God's hands. The Word of God had absorbed him like a towel absorbs water.

About five years after Jeremiah's call to service, when he was approximately 25 years old, in the year 621 B.C., a remarkable event took place in Judah, an event that also focuses on the Word of God.

Josiah, the boy-king, was no longer a boy. He too was in his mid-20s. His reform movement had been going on for five or six years.

In the countryside around Jerusalem, idolatry had become a tradition. Priests had been setting up local shrines. Pagan worship had even invaded the temple in Jerusalem.

That's where Josiah began his housecleaning—right in the temple. He sought to restore the pure worship of Jehovah. And in the process of spring housecleaning, workmen uncovered the ancient scroll of the Law, probably the Book of Deuteronomy.

How easy it is to lose God's Word in the clutter of things!

The scroll was brought to King Josiah and the youthful king read God's Word with excitement and expectation. But the Scripture struck home to Josiah. In spite of all his reforms, he saw how far short his nation had fallen from meeting God's requirements. In anguish, he tore his royal robes and sought God's forgiveness.

If Jeremiah needed any confirmation that the Word of God was powerful, this was it. His monarch was bowing before it.

What a powerful secret weapon the Word of God was, and is, and will be forever.

Perhaps the problem is that we keep it too secret. Perhaps the problem is that we have lost its power in the rubble of things.

3

The Start, the Finish, and the In-Between

Jeremiah 2:1—3:5; 11:1-17; 3:6—6:30

I stood alongside the high school track. Next to me was a teenager on crutches, the disabled ace of the local cross-country squad. We watched silently as the runners loped around the oval track and then disappeared one by one behind the school building. As they went out of sight, I was alarmed to note that none of our men were in front. Five of our opponents were far ahead.

I looked at my friend with some concern. He must have read it on my face. Even with him disabled, our school had a strong team. I couldn't understand why the opposition was so far ahead of us.

My friend was not known to be talkative and I didn't expect a voluminous reply. In fact, I was surprised to get a response at all. But he did say something and it was significant. It was simply this: "It's easy to start; it's hard to finish." As a cross-country runner, he knew it only too well.

Quite a few minutes later, the runners emerged from the shadows that hung around the other side of the school. Leading the way were four runners wearing the colors of the local school.

"It's easy to start; it's hard to finish."

I've always found more joy in starting things than in finishing things. Jeremiah found it to be true. So did the Israelites. So did the Ephesians. So did a man named Demas.

The Forsakers

I don't know exactly what Demas' problem was. He had been a bright young convert, and the Apostle Paul seemed to think of him as one with considerable promise. You might have called him a protegé of the apostle. Paul spoke of Demas in the same breath with Mark and Luke (Phile. 24).

During Paul's first Roman imprisonment when he penned several of his epistles, he was fortunate to have Demas by his side. But then something happened. After the first lap, Demas seemed to be leading the field; but when he is mentioned again, he is an "also-ran." Paul remarks sadly that Demas had forsaken him (2 Tim. 4:9-10).

Why had he forsaken Paul? No one really knows Demas' heart, but Paul commented that Demas had fallen in love with the present world (v. 10). In another place Paul urges believers to run, looking unto Jesus. Demas had started looking in the wrong direction.

There is no indication that Demas flatly denied the faith or that he rejected the doctrines of Scripture. He simply became enamored with the present "age." He no longer viewed things from the perspective of eternity.

The Christians in the church of Ephesus are another case study. In the Book of Revelation, the risen Christ says sternly to the church of Ephesus, "I have this against you that you have left your first love" (Rev. 2:4, NASB). The honeymoon had ended, the thrill had gone out of the marriage.

Something had happened; something had gone sour. William Cowper once wrote:

> Where is the blessedness I knew
> When first I saw the Lord?
> Where is the soul-refreshing view
> Of Jesus and His Word?

The Ephesians might have asked the same questions.

A few years earlier, the Christians in Ephesus had been

known for their love, not only for God, but also for one another. Paul had written to them, commending them for their "love for all the saints" (Eph. 1:15). But a generation had passed, and no longer were the Christians of Ephesus characterized by love. Something had gone wrong. It was business as usual in Ephesus. The Ephesian believers were still doing things for God; but they had lost something, something extremely important—love.

And then there were the residents of Judah in the time of Jeremiah. There was no doubt but that the Children of Israel had started the race well. They had crossed the Red Sea in grand style. Joshua had led them across the Jordan River, and then in a glorious victory had conquered Jericho. But that was now ancient history.

Cisterns in the Sand

As Jeremiah preached and later dictated the second chapter of his prophecy, he wasn't thinking of running, but of getting married. There is something powerfully poignant about Jeremiah's words:

> I remember when you said, "I do": I remember how you said you loved Me at our wedding; I remember our honeymoon, how you went with Me to a place you did not know. I brought you out of a wilderness into a garden, out of a desert, into a paradise, out of a hovel of poverty, into a mansion of plenty. . . . But you have polluted My land; you have defiled everything I have lovingly given you. I even provided you with a fountain of sparkling pure water, but you walked away from it. Instead you dug for yourself a cistern in the sand. (See Jer. 2:1-13.)

That's a free translation, but it gives you an idea of the force of Jeremiah's words. Speaking for God, Jeremiah combs every figure of speech to get his point across. He calls the people redeemed slaves who have returned to slavery (2:14); he calls them a noble red sorek grape that has degenerated into a wild vine (v. 21); he calls them wild animals—a camel and an ass in heat (vv. 23-24).

And then come the saddest lines of all: "You have said, 'It's no use. I love strangers, and after them I will go'" (v. 25). Apostasy runs a strange pattern. It promises so much and delivers so little. It usually begins with moral aberration and meanders into theological defection.

What you are doing doesn't make sense, God says through Jeremiah. You're exchanging the Almighty God of the universe for a bargain-basement Barbie doll. You're exchanging a diamond ring for a daisy chain, the original Gutenberg Bible for a scratch pad. Instead of fresh water from a sparkling fountain, you build cisterns in the sand. No, it doesn't make sense.

In *The Land and the Book*, J.A. Thompson describes Palestinian cisterns: "The best cisterns, even those in solid rock, are strangely liable to crack, and are a most unreliable source of supply of that absolutely indispensable article, water; and if, by constant care, they are made to hold, yet the water, collected from clay roofs or from marly soil, has the color of weak soapsuds, the taste of the earth or the stable, is full of worms, and in the hour of greatest need it utterly fails. Who but a fool positive or one gone mad in love with filth, would exchange the sweet, wholesome stream of a living fountain for such an uncertain mixture of nastiness and vermin?"

Five Steps Down
Perhaps what surprised Jeremiah the most was not that his people had forsaken the Lord, but that they had no awe of Him. They took His forgiveness for granted. He was always there to come home to.

Thus, in Jeremiah's mind, there was a downward progression and he saw the steps this way:

STEP ONE: Forsaking God, the spring of living water;
STEP TWO: Going after other gods; digging cisterns in the sand;
STEP THREE: Having lost an awe for God and His justice;
STEP FOUR: Having lost any shame for sin;

STEP FIVE: Committing themselves to follow other gods. Those downward steps are not unique to the Israelites nor to Jeremiah's lifetime. The same steps are taken by many today. You may begin to forsake God by neglecting His Word, by being so busy with other things that you don't spend time with Him in prayer and in private devotion, by becoming careless in your attendance at services of worship and praise with your brothers and sisters in Christ.

It often starts, however, with your attitude toward the Book. D.L. Moody said about the Bible, "This Book will keep you from sin, or sin will keep you from this Book." Jeremiah knew that too. When people neglected God's Word, when they stopped drinking from the stream of living water, they started digging their own cisterns in the sand.

It may have started as a temporary fascination, a momentary allurement, but when you found you could get away with it, you started digging the cistern deeper and more permanently. The deeper you dug, the more you realized the shallowness of it all. And what started as a hobby became a career.

For the Israelites, it began as a sideline—God and Baal together. Two gods must be better than one. At first, Baal was a passing fancy, but soon it became more than that. What began as a fascination and a fantasy, they began to follow.

And as Baal became more a part of their daily lives, Jehovah became less. It always works that way. No longer did they fear Jehovah; no longer were they afraid that they would face punishment for their sins. Then, having submerged their fear of the living God, they lost their sense of shame and plunged headlong into their commitment to foreign gods.

Shallow Revival

It's hard to pinpoint the dates on chapters 2 through 6 of Jeremiah. These five chapters consist of two of Jeremiah's earliest sermons. The first covers 2:1—3:5 and the second goes from 3:6—6:30. Between the fifth and sixth verses of chapter 3, something very momentous took place. It is here that I would place the discovery of the scroll of the Law by

King Josiah (mentioned in the last chapter), as contained in 2 Kings 23 and the first few verses of Jeremiah 11. The chronology goes something like this: In 631 B.C. young Josiah, now age 16, "began to seek after the God of David" (2 Chron. 34:3, KJV.) Four years later, in 627 B.C., he began his purge of idols from Jerusalem, and probably around 623 B.C. Jeremiah began his preaching mission in Jerusalem.

God had told him, "Go and proclaim in the hearing of Jerusalem, 'Thus saith the Lord.' " And so Jeremiah commuted back and forth between his suburban village of Anathoth and the capital city of Jerusalem, preaching God's message.

Then in about 621 B.C. Josiah ordered workmen to repair the temple, and in the process of the repair, they discovered the ancient scroll, probably the Book of Deuteronomy (2 Kings 22:8). When the book was read to King Josiah, the monarch was dismayed and rent his clothes (v. 11). No doubt, the warnings in the Book of Deuteronomy were sterner than he had imagined. "Great is the wrath of the Lord that is kindled against us," he mourned (v. 13, KJV).

Was it too late to repent? Could anything be done to prevent the calamities that God had predicted?

To get his answers, young Josiah didn't turn to his court prophets. Most of the kings of Judah had employed court prophets, but these were mostly yes men. They had lost the respect of any God-fearing people, and the king seldom asked them for advice unless he wanted his own inclinations confirmed.

Josiah didn't turn to Jeremiah either. Jeremiah was still in his mid-20s and he was a newcomer. Instead Josiah turned to a prophetess named Huldah. The wife of a minor temple official, she was enough of an insider to be respected, but still had enough independence to be trusted.

With bold, "Thus saith the Lord" strokes, Huldah underlined the message of Deuteronomy (and the message of Jeremiah). Because the people had turned away from God, His wrath would be "kindled against the place, and shall not be quenched" (v. 17, KJV).

That autumn, in conjunction with the Feast of Tabernacles, Josiah called the people of his kingdom together in a covenant renewal ceremony. Just as the Book of Deuteronomy itself was a renewal of the covenant given by God at Sinai, so Josiah asked the people to once again reaffirm their covenant relationship with God.

Standing by a pillar in the temple, Josiah read the covenant promised by God in Deuteronomy. The king read both the blessings and the threatened curses. When he finished reading, all the people solemnly gave their allegiance to the covenant. You can be sure that Jeremiah was one of the first to say his Amen to it.

It must have been a moving experience for Jeremiah. At first, his response must have been almost euphoric. Was this a genuine revival taking place? Did the people really mean it when they said Amen to God's Law?

The Long Way Back

During his public preaching, Jeremiah hadn't noticed much visible response. But he might have wondered whether his preaching had softened the people's hearts a bit and prepared them for Josiah's reading of God's Word. Regardless of whether the people had meant their Amens or not, Jeremiah had a mandate from God to reinforce it, to make sure that the people did not forget what they had promised.

This is where Jeremiah 11:1-8 fits in. In these verses God makes a mini-covenant with Jeremiah, and once again Jeremiah responds, "So be it, Lord." His responsibility was now to go throughout the land and to roam the streets of Jerusalem reminding the people of their covenant promise. What he preached was probably the sermon outlined in Jeremiah 3—6.

In these chapters you find a new string on Jeremiah's instrument. "God is merciful," Jeremiah shouts through the villages and hamlets of Judah. "Return to Him and He will forgive." God is a judge, yes. God is holy and righteous, yes. But He still loves you. He is still your husband.

In his first message (Jer. 2:1—3:5), the young prophet sounded as if there were no road back. But now, he brings hope. However, as Jeremiah traveled throughout the land, he made a very unpleasant discovery. The farther he got from Jerusalem, the more he saw how deeply ingrained idolatry had become in the lives of his people. The people who had said Amen when King Josiah read Deuteronomy returned to their idols when they got home. "Judah," Jeremiah concluded sadly, "did not return to God with all her heart, but only in pretense."

Even so, Jeremiah said, God had provided a way back. The first step was the desire to return. "Yes, we will come to You, for You are the Lord our God" (3:22). The second step was the recognition of sin's deception and shame. "Surely the idolatrous commotion on the hills and mountains is a deception. . . . From our youth shameful gods have consumed the fruits of our fathers' labor" (vv. 23-24). The third step was the acknowledgment of personal responsibility for sin. "We have sinned . . . we have not obeyed" (v. 25).

But the people were not returning to God. And in spite of all that King Josiah was trying to do, the people were really no different than before.

As Jeremiah toured the land and then returned to roam the narrow streets of Jerusalem again, his heart was broken. The realization was almost more than he could stand. The discovery of the scroll of the Law had raised false hopes. The thought that his preaching had paved the way to a national revival was a foolish fantasy. He had thought that the coming catastrophe could be averted, but he realized that God's judgment was inevitable.

Of course, the priests and the temple prophets were still saying that everything would be all right. Even the priests in Anathoth seemed to think that the Millennium was just around the corner. But Jeremiah knew better. And it distressed him. In agony he cried out to God, "Ah, Lord God, You have deceived us" (see 4:10).

But the fault wasn't God's. God answered that the people

themselves were responsible for the coming calamity. "Your own conduct and actions have brought this upon you" (4:18). Then Jeremiah, identifying himself with his people and the nation he loved, began to realize as never before that disaster was coming down from above like an avalanche and there was no getting out of its way. He groaned, "Oh my anguish, my anguish! I writhe in pain. Oh, the agony of my heart!" (v. 19)

He laments his people's proclivity to sin. "They are wise to do evil, but to do good they have no knowledge" (4:22, KJV). He envisions a desolate fate and his poetry emerges as some of the most memorable in the entire Bible:

I looked at the earth,
    and it was formless and empty;
And at the heavens,
    and their light was gone.
I looked at the mountains,
    and they were quaking;
all the hills were swaying.
I looked, and there were no people;
    every bird in the sky had flown away.
I looked, and the fruitful land was a desert;
    all its towns lay in ruins
before the Lord, before His fierce anger (vv. 23-26).

"Turn Back to God!"

Maybe, Jeremiah mused, it was only the poor peasants in the rural areas who were violating God's Law. Maybe they could be excused because they didn't know any better (5:4). So Jeremiah checked out the religious leaders in Jerusalem; to his dismay he found that they were just as bad as the peasants.

These leaders who should have been the closest to God seemed to be the coldest to spiritual truth. They didn't believe Jeremiah. They didn't acknowledge their sin; they didn't think God would do anything about it. Instead of listening to God's Word, they found it offensive. It seemed that everyone was living for themselves. "All are greedy for gain," Jeremiah said. "All practice deceit" (6:13).

Just because Josiah had found the Book of the Law in Jerusalem and because Assyria was not currently menacing them from the North, the people talked as if peace would be their portion forever. "Peace, peace," Jeremiah said sarcastically. "But there is no peace" (v. 14, NASB). You may not be able to see it, but an army is coming from the north and will devastate Jerusalem.

That was Jeremiah's message; it seemed ridiculous at the time. The people must have laughed at him. This was hardly the time to warn against an invasion of foreign troops.

"Get back on the right path again," Jeremiah continued (v. 16). "Don't be spiritual dropouts."

But no one listened.

Jeremiah was caught in the middle. At times he was trying to defend his people against God's wrath. At times he was trying to find excuses for their conduct. But sooner or later, when arguing with God, he always ran out of excuses.

Then, when the people refused to listen to God's message—not only the peasants, but also the leaders—Jeremiah's frustration reached its limit. "I'm full of the wrath of God," he exclaimed. "I'm ready to explode" (v. 11). No, Jeremiah didn't possess the patience of Job, and certainly not the patience of God. But what he lacked in patience, he made up for in perseverance.

At this point, it would have been easy for Jeremiah to say, "I can't take it any more. This is tearing me apart. It doesn't do me any good to preach. No one listens. I think I've done my job. I've completed a preaching tour of the land as You told me, but I accomplished nothing. So now let me go back to Anathoth. Lord, let me quit."

But God didn't let Jeremiah quit. His work—though unproductive and though unpleasant—wasn't done yet.

It's not how you start; it's how you finish. And Jeremiah's race had just begun.

4

But, Lord, I Don't Want To Be an Object Lesson

Jeremiah 11:18—12:6; 16:1-9; 15:10-21

"A man in sorrow is in general far nearer God than a man in joy. Gladness may make a man forget his thanksgiving; misery drives him to his prayer." So spoke the noted Scottish preacher-writer George MacDonald.

Aloneness and loneliness are not the same. You can be alone and not be lonely, and you can be surrounded by a cast of thousands and be the loneliest person in the world.

Of course, loneliness comes in many shapes and sizes and it afflicts all kinds of people. Many people are sick emotionally because of loneliness and others are sick physically because of it. Perhaps the most severe forms of loneliness are experienced by people who are unusually sensitive. They love deeply, but no one—it seems—returns their love.

It's true that some lonely people don't have immediate reasons for their loneliness. Their feelings may have deep psychological roots. But Jeremiah, whatever else you might say about him, had some valid reasons to be lonely.

Start Packing
Let's pick up the story in Jeremiah 11:18. The year may be 619 or 620 B.C. Jeremiah has probably just returned from a

preaching tour throughout the country, and now he is preaching in his home town of Anathoth. His message is the same as it has been elsewhere: "God's Word must be obeyed. The local shrines must be torn down. False gods must be forsaken. The people must worship Jehovah at the temple in Jerusalem."

At this time, Anathoth was filled with displaced priests. Ever since Priest Abiathar had sided with Absalom in his insurrection against King David and had been banished to Anathoth, the suburban town had been inhabited by disenfranchised priests. So when it became the vogue to set up local shrines, many of the unemployed priests of Anathoth set up shop in their hometown.

Then Jeremiah brought home the same message that local shrines must be torn down; worship must be in Jerusalem. Obviously, this meant that half the town would be standing in unemployment lines. It was like advocating the closing down of the automobile factories in Detroit, the steel mills in Pittsburgh, or the aircraft industry in Seattle. In a word, Jeremiah was taking bread off of his neighbors' tables.

At least, that's how it seemed to the townsfolk of Anathoth. Jeremiah was a traitor. It would have been bad enough for someone from Jerusalem to urge the shutting down of the local shrines. But Jeremiah was a local boy. Needless to say, the people of Anathoth were angry—livid with rage. So angry, in fact, that they plotted to kill the young prophet.

When and how Jeremiah discovered the plot is not known. Apparently when he arrived in Anathoth, he had been greeted warmly enough. His family and relatives spoke "fair words" to him (12:6). "I did not know it was against me they devised schemes," Jeremiah says. "I was like a gentle lamb led to the slaughter," he says, recalling the famous words of a previous prophet (Isa. 53).

But soon Jeremiah realized that he was the object of a whispering campaign. He brought it out into the open, confronting his neighbors to their faces. There was no denying it. Their response: "Stop prophesying or else." And there was no question what the "or else" meant (Jer. 11:21).

Why, Lord?

It was a shock, a deep traumatic bruising of Jeremiah's nervous system. These were his neighbors and friends. These were the fellows and girls with whom he had grown up. In fact, even his brothers and cousins were involved (12:6).

He had returned from his prophetic tour throughout Judah a bit discouraged and disappointed that his countrymen weren't following the lead of their king. Perhaps he had higher hopes for the response he would get in his hometown. But now, even in Anathoth, he was *persona non grata*. And not only was he "not wanted," he was threatened with murder—by the people he assumed were his friends.

Several hundred years later, Jesus must have felt the same way when He returned from a speaking tour and entered the synagogue in His hometown of Nazareth. His hometown friends took Him out to the brow of a hill to kill Him.

All sorts of emotions must have cascaded on Jeremiah. He must have felt trapped. If he didn't stop preaching, he would probably be killed by his neighbors. If he did stop preaching, he would face the wrath of God. If he chose Course A, he would have the friendship of One—God. If he chose Course B, he would have the friendship of many—the citizens of Anathoth.

For Jeremiah, it had to be Course A. His only decision was when to pack his bags and leave Anathoth. That wasn't a hard decision either. The sooner the better.

The first several verses of chapter 12 may have been composed as Jeremiah was trudging, perhaps in the middle of the night, from Anathoth to Jerusalem. He was talking to his one Friend. What he couldn't understand—and here he sounded a bit like Job—was why God allows the wicked to prosper.

It would be much easier to preach God's message calling people to repent, if God would do His job of zapping the evil-doers with thunderbolts every day or two. But that wasn't

happening. The evildoers were living in ease and comfort. It was Jeremiah, friendless, who was the outcast. Why, Lord? God's answer wasn't exactly satisfying:
> If you have raced with men on foot
> and they have worn you out,
> how can you compete with horses?
> If you stumble on an easy road,
> how will you manage in the thickets of the Jordan?

Did the Lord think it was nothing for Jeremiah to be run out of Anathoth? Had the Lord considered it an "ordinary thing" for him to be the subject of a murder plot in his own hometown? Yet, as grim as it was, the answer was simply this: "Jeremiah, if you think you've experienced trouble, you haven't seen anything yet."

Be an Object Lesson

Exactly *when* God dropped the next bombshell on Jeremiah is not known, but you can read about it in Jeremiah 16:1-9. Jeremiah was living in Jerusalem by this time. He had moved permanently out of Anathoth. Living in Jerusalem may have gotten him away from the murder plot, but it did nothing to help his loneliness.

Then came God's next message. Jeremiah must have been about 30 years old when God said, "You shall not take a wife and you shall not have children." For a red-blooded Hebrew man who was already struggling with loneliness, this wasn't an easy matter to handle. A man's worth was measured by the number of his children.

We have other yardsticks to measure a man's worth and most of them are just as erroneous as counting his children. A man may be measured by his job, his salary, his home, or his education; a woman may be measured by her beauty, her homemaking, her job, or her church or community involvement. But none of these are of most importance to God.

Why couldn't Jeremiah marry? Because his life was to be an object lesson for Israel. Children born during the next 30 years would face disease and famine, pestilence and sword. They would be taken into captivity and face deep emotional pain. As another object lesson, God told Jeremiah that he was forbidden to participate in the social times of his fellow Israelites. He couldn't go to parties, weddings, or banquets. He couldn't even attend a funeral. And to a Jew of that day, a good funeral was looked forward to as much as a good party.

But God said that Israel would soon be suffering His divine wrath and wouldn't be in the mood to celebrate anything. So Jeremiah, as the object lesson, had to forgo good times as well.

Jeremiah must have wished that God would have chosen someone else to be His object lesson. A sensitive man, friendless, run out of his hometown, despised by his neighbors, hated by relatives, forbidden by God to get married and have a family, forbidden also to attend any social events in Jerusalem—that was Jeremiah. No wonder he has been called the "weeping prophet."

"Poor Me"
This is probably where Jeremiah blurts out his confession found in Jeremiah 15:10-18. "Woe is me!" Jeremiah shouted out to God. "I wish I had never been born. Everyone hates me, even though I have interceded with You for them. . . . I didn't go to parties and banquets. I didn't attend weddings. Instead, I sat alone." Poor Jeremiah.

Lonely, but more than lonely. His loneliness has brought him to uncertainty. He has served God faithfully, but now he wonders if God will "come through" for him. Or will God be like a "deceitful brook," one that promises much, but is dry for 10 months of the year? Earlier he had charged that the Israelites were digging "cisterns in the sand." Was he, God's ordained prophet, now suggesting that God Himself was a cistern in the sand?

It's amazing what we say to God when we are confused and distressed. But it's even more amazing to see how gracious God is in letting us vent our confusion in His presence. God likes to respond to honest prayers, no matter how off-base they are. At least Jeremiah was being honest.

Jeremiah's loneliness had given him "I" trouble. In 15:15-18 (NASB), he refers to the first-person singular 18 times. He had made himself the central character in the drama, rather than a member of the supporting cast. His personal concerns had become more important than the providential commission. Daily pursuits had usurped the place of the divine purpose.

God's response to this complaint of Jeremiah was no easier on the prophet than God's first rejoinder when He had told him, "If you think this is bad, you don't know what bad is." This time God says to Jeremiah, "Repent."

That wasn't easy for the prophet to swallow. After all, he had been telling the people to repent, the people who had been playing around with idols, who had forgotten what the Ten Commandments were all about, who had forsaken the worship of Jehovah. They *needed* to repent; it was very obvious that they did. But Jeremiah, in this darkest of hours, needed to repent too.

You might think that this was rather stern, even uncaring, for God to handle His sensitive prophet this way. Maybe it was stern, but Jeremiah needed a jolt. And when we start feeling sorry for ourselves, we sometimes need a jolt more than we need sympathy.

A Promise from God

Along with the call to repentance, God gave Jeremiah a promise of restoration. The *Jerusalem Bible* puts it this way: "If you come back, I will take you back into My service." Southern Baptist commentator James Leo Green aptly says, "When a servant of God is in the throes of doubt and distress, the real question becomes: Will he run away? or, Will he stick and struggle through? The only way out is through a deeper surrender to God and a more sincere service of God. A greater commitment leads to greater certainty" (*The Broadman Bible Commentary*, vol. 6, Broadman Press, p. 96).

God was calling Jeremiah to a greater commitment. In

return, God promised that He would make Jeremiah to be a bronze wall which would not break down under any onslaught. The walls of Jerusalem would collapse, but God's bronze wall would never crumble.

Often young people—and sometimes older people as well—commit themselves to God without knowing what it means to follow the Lord. Then, after some difficult times, they may come to a time of crisis when a deeper commitment is required. This was that kind of time for Jeremiah. A.S. Peake remarks: "Unshrinking obedience, rendered without hesitation or complaint, that is the condition imposed by God upon those who aspire to the high dignity of His service. And the reward of service faithfully rendered is, as in the Parable of the Pounds, more service."

When Jeremiah got back on his feet again, he uttered the words, "O Lord, my strength and my stronghold, my refuge in the day of trouble" (16:19, RSV). Jeremiah was still aware of his own weakness, but now he became more aware of God's strength.

Of course, Jeremiah was still a lonely man. He certainly wasn't surrounded by intimate friends. But even in his loneliness God made him an object lesson to his people. Later, Jeremiah began the Book of Lamentations with the words, "How lonely sits the city that was full of people! . . . She weeps bitterly in the night, tears on her cheeks" (Lam. 1:1-2, RSV). Jeremiah knew what loneliness was all about.

Loneliness, of course, is not the same as aloneness. Aloneness relates to external circumstances; loneliness relates to internal feelings. It is healthy for us to have times of aloneness, but God doesn't want us to be afflicted with deep loneliness. Too much aloneness can bring about loneliness. God knew this when He created Adam. "It is not good for the man to be alone," He said, and then made Eve as Adam's companion (Gen. 2:18).

Loneliness can best be cured by love. Those who know how to give and receive love can generally overcome the assaults of loneliness. In his book *What You Should Know about Emo-*

tions and Mental Health, Paul Keating tells of a woman who "woke up one morning with the realization that she felt she had no one in the world who cared whether she was alive or dead. It mattered not to anyone if she took another breath. Total despair and an overdose of sleeping pills were narrowly avoided by the poignantly discovered fact that her two cats would not be fed if she did not get up and go to work and earn a living."

Several years ago, an anonymous writer in *Eternity* magazine (Nov. 1973) spoke about her struggles with loneliness: "It is too simple to say that loneliness is an emotional sickness. Nor should we say that it is simply the result of alienation and our sinful nature. Sometimes it is thrust upon us by birth, by circumstances of life, by accident or by a combination of these. Often it is the result of having an inhuman burden to bear."

The writer goes on to say that many Christians "are lonely but don't admit it." It may break out in a hypercritical attitude, in a domineering spirit, or a biting tongue. It may be seen in a sense of worthlessness as the lonely person constantly depreciates himself.

What's the solution? First, you must recognize who God is. He is both great and good. He is both omnipotent and loving. When you grasp (and appropriate) the character of the Almighty God, you have taken the first step out of the pit of loneliness.

Second, you must accept what God has given you. This is not resignation to fate; this is acceptance of the will of a wise and loving God.

Third, you must see the subtle snares of loneliness. It's easy to get completely wrapped up in self and that is disastrous for a healthy Christian life.

Fourth, you need to take positive action to help you cope with loneliness and perhaps to restore a life of service to God.

Some suggested courses of possible action are to get busy, even though it may not seem like significant service; to seek to understand yourself and your problems of loneliness; to develop the art of communicating with others on a deep level; to discover the gifts that God has given you to serve Him; and finally to seek out those who are needier than you are, and then to minister to them.

Interestingly enough, Jeremiah took many of these same steps—and he stopped being "poor" Jeremiah. He was rich, for he had God, and that was more than his townsmen had.

5

Hand Me My
Security Blanket

Jeremiah 7–10; 26

'What makes you feel secure?"

"Do you mean nationally or personally?"

"Both."

"Well, I feel good about the security of our nation if we have a strong military, if we have made some meaningful alliances with friendly countries, and if we're working on our relations with the others."

"What about the moral fiber of the people?"

"Oh, yeah, that's important too. That should be included on the list. If people don't have the moral stamina to stand up for what's right, the rest won't matter."

"What makes you feel personally secure?"

"Having a job, a home, a family, some money in the bank. Good health, that sort of thing."

"What about church?"

"Of course. I guess I took that for granted. Church is very important to my feeling of security. When things go wrong at church, my whole world starts to shake a bit."

"Do you think God ever shakes up a person's security?"

"Sure, He does. He tests it, you know. But then there's Romans 8:28 and lots of other verses. And, of course, that's

why we have so many Christian counselors around these days."

"Why is that?"

"So that when you start feeling a little bit insecure, they start making you feel secure again."

"I see. So insecurity is always bad; security is always good."

"Exactly."

"Hmmm. I wonder what Jeremiah would have thought of all that."

Everything's Going Our Way

The citizens of Judah were feeling very secure in 609 B.C., and there seemed to be good reason for it. There was also good reason for them to ignore the alarmist notes sounded by that out-of-tune Prophet Jeremiah. After all, the kingdom of Assyria which had been oppressing and exacting tribute from Judah for over 200 years had fallen. The dragon's fangs had been pulled.

About the time that Jeremiah had his prophetic call, the Assyrian emperor Ashurbanipal died; Assyria went rapidly downhill from then on. And in 612 B.C., when Assyria's capital city of Nineveh fell to the Babylonians, that virtually finished Assyria.

Jeremiah went on preaching and calling people to repentance, but his words fell on deaf ears. Jeremiah seemed to have the knack of preaching the wrong message at the wrong time in the wrong place. At least, that's what the people thought. Earlier he had called people to repentance in a time of Josiah's national revival. The Word of God had been found and people were once again going to the temple in Jerusalem. Now Jeremiah was talking about danger from the north when there seemed to be less danger from the north than there had been for centuries.

Yes, the people of Judah were feeling secure. They had everything going for them—a godly king, a temple in Jerusalem that was their pride and joy, and a long-time enemy which had just bitten the dust. Even King Josiah was feeling secure, too secure. Along with his people, Josiah must have dreamt that he would be able to bring his nation back to its former glories. It may have been one reason why Jeremiah never climbed into royal favor. Jeremiah seemed to be a "Gloomy Gus." Josiah, on the other hand, was blind to what was going on behind his back, underneath the table, and around the corner. What he saw was the surface. Jeremiah, with divinely aided insight, saw beneath the surface.

Thus it happened in 609 b.c. that when the Egyptian army was marching north toward Assyria, Josiah, foolishly trying to stop them, got in the way of an Egyptian arrow. His 30-year reign was abruptly and tragically halted. The entire nation mourned.

Josiah's son, Jehoahaz, reigned only three months before the Egyptians, riled by the upstart Judeans, deposed him. Then, an elder brother, Jehoiakim, took the throne, promising to pay Egypt heavy taxes.

The events of 609 b.c. must have been a blow to the pride of Judah—good King Josiah slain in battle, a popular son Jehoahaz deposed by the Egyptians, and another son Jehoiakim, not so popular, installed in his place only when he promised that he would play the game according to Egypt's ground rules.

But the people quickly got over the shock. Soon it was business as usual in Judah. Jehoiakim was trying to make the people forget the trauma by launching grandiose building programs, extending his royal palace and other governmental structures. At first, he didn't tell them that they would have to pay not only taxes to Egypt, but also extra taxes for his building projects.

It's amazing what resilience the people had. Of course, they were confident that God wouldn't allow His city of Jerusalem to fall. Of course, He wouldn't, not as long as His house, His temple, was in it. God just wouldn't do a thing like that, would He?

So the people's security was shaken, but not smashed. In fact, Jehoiakim even promised to give them more security.

After all, he came to the throne with Egypt's blessing. With God, the temple, and Egypt all on the side of Judah, they could feel secure indeed.

No More "Power to Blush"

Shortly after Jehoiakim came to the throne, Jeremiah began preaching again. And once again, he seemed like the wrong prophet in the wrong place with the wrong message at the wrong time.

The story picks up in two different places in the Book of Jeremiah. Chapter 7 gives his sermon; chapter 26 gives the results of the sermon. The time was either late in 609 B.C. or early in 608 B.C. Jeremiah was now in his late 30s.

One of Jeremiah's perennial problems was that he was not the only prophet in Judah. To complicate matters, the other prophets did not agree with what he was saying. And if God's message were to be decided by a majority vote, Jeremiah would have lost by a landslide. Besides that, the other prophets were more popular than Jeremiah—more popular with the people, more popular with the priests (and that may have hurt Jeremiah because he came from a priestly tribe), and certainly more popular with the new king who hadn't inherited any of his father's godly concerns.

Jeremiah called them false prophets, but to the people they made good sense. According to Jeremiah's competition, God had promised an everlasting kingdom to David. Jeremiah couldn't disagree with that. The false prophets also proclaimed that Jehovah had chosen the temple in Jerusalem (and particularly the holy place in the temple) as the focus of His earthly abode. Jeremiah couldn't disagree with that either. Therefore it was only logical that God would never allow His temple nor His city to fall into the hands of the enemy. Right, Jeremiah?

But that's where Jeremiah disagreed, even though the false prophets seemed to make sense.

The false prophets had history on their side as well. They recalled what had happened in the days of Hezekiah when

Jerusalem had been surrounded by the Assyrians. God miraculously smote the enemy and His chosen city was spared. The false prophets must have loved to tell that story. But Jeremiah countered that it wouldn't happen this time.

Inside the temple, the false prophets were assuring the people that all was secure. Outside, Jeremiah positioned himself at one of the temple gates and preached his best-known sermon. "You can't find real security in the temple," said Jeremiah. "Real security can be found only in God Himself."

The temple had become a good-luck charm. The people were going through the motions, and that was good enough for the priest and the false prophets. But it wasn't good enough for Jeremiah and it wasn't good enough for God. Jeremiah was taking all the security blankets off the Israelites and one by one he was ripping them to shreds.

"God demands a clean heart, and unless your heart is clean, the temple isn't going to do you any good." But Jeremiah said that the people's imported incense and cane made the temple stink to high heaven. Even the temple sacrifices, Jeremiah said, were not as important as obedience. The first thing God commanded when He brought the Israelites out of Egypt was not the observance of sacrifices, but obedience to His commandments.

Sin was becoming more blatant. It seemed that the people didn't care, and they had the notion that God didn't care either as long as they kept coming to the temple with their sacrifices. They had divorced ritual from meaning, worship from practice, and the sanctuary from the marketplace. F.B. Meyer says that the people had lost "the power to blush."

The problem wasn't that they were sinners; the temple sacrifices were established for the purpose of reminding people that they were sinners and then of helping them put their sin under the blood of the lamb. But the people had sublimated their sense of sinfulness and thus had forgotten what the temple was really for.

Then Jeremiah delivered the real shocker. He reminded

them that when the tabernacle was first set up in the Promised Land, it was located in Shiloh. Now Shiloh was demolished. Jerusalem, Jeremiah said, would be laid waste even as Shiloh was.

That sounded like heresy to them. "The temple of the Lord, the temple of the Lord, the temple of the Lord," they cried as if they were cheerleaders at a high school football game (Jer. 7:4). But if it were a game, Jeremiah knew that the time was running out, the game was in its final quarter, and the spectators didn't even know what was happening on the field.

Shredded Security Blankets

Chapters 8—10 contain sections of various sermons preached by Jeremiah. Possibly the sermons were delivered over a period of several weeks in 608 B.C. In-between each sermon, it would seem, Jeremiah went home and talked to God about it, sometimes complaining, sometimes not understanding, sometimes weeping, and sometimes even feeling a bit insecure.

Yes, Jeremiah had some pangs of insecurity too. It was understandable. He had been run out of his hometown, had been disowned by his family, had been ordered by God to remain single, and had been completely unsuccessful as a prophet in getting people to heed his message. Yet his only insecurity resided in himself. He was doing a job that he did not feel he was cut out to do, and that gave him some occasions for insecurity. But at the same time he knew that he was ultimately secure as long as he obeyed the will of God. And unlike his people, that's what he kept on doing.

In these several chapters containing bits and pieces of Jeremiah's temple sermons, you find some of the most quoted verses of his entire prophecy. Jesus Himself quoted Jeremiah 7:11 as He cleansed the temple: "My house shall be called a house of prayer, but you have made it a den of thieves" (Matt. 21:13, NKJV). The authorities didn't care for the verse in Jesus' day any more than they did in the time of Jeremiah.

Jeremiah 8:11: "Peace, peace, they say, when there is no peace." Jeremiah was aiming that barb at the false prophets and priests who were leading cheers on the sidelines. Jeremiah 8:20: "The harvest is passed, the summer has ended, and we are not saved." This is one of Jeremiah's laments inserted in between bits of his message. The harvest may have referred to Josiah's revival movement; the summer may have referred to Jeremiah's prophetic ministry. Neither produced lasting results.

Jeremiah 8:22: "Is there no balm in Gilead? Is there no physician there?" Jeremiah is still lamenting. Gilead, across the Jordan River, was known for a healing ointment derived from the resin of a native tree. Jeremiah was asking God in behalf of his people for a miracle cure for their incurable disease.

Jeremiah 9:1: "Oh that my head were waters, and mine eyes a fountain of tears, that I might weep day and night for the slain of the daughter of my people!" (KJV) Here's where Jeremiah got the nickname of the weeping prophet.

Jeremiah 10:23: "O Lord, I know that the way of man is not in himself: it is not in man that walketh to direct his steps" (KJV). The sensitive prophet realized man's limitations in avoiding the snares of sin.

But back to the matter of security. Obviously, Jeremiah felt his people's sense of security was wrongly based. Even Josiah's discovery of God's Word would not avert the coming disaster. God's Word needs to be *done*, not merely possessed. Perhaps Jeremiah sums up the entire matter of security most succinctly when he says: "Let not the wise man glory in his wisdom, neither let the mighty man glory in his might, let not the rich man glory in his riches; but let him that glorieth glory in this, that he understandeth and knoweth Me, that I am the Lord which exercise loving-kindess, judgment, and righteousness, in the earth: for in these things I delight"(9:23-24, KJV).

Jeremiah's main point was the false sense of security that wisdom, riches, and power can give us. And having said this, Jeremiah had shredded the last security blankets that the Israelites possessed.

It's strange how little we have learned since the time of

Jeremiah. We try to patch up those same security blankets and hold them close to ourselves. When you ask people what they need to feel secure, the answers come back much the same as they would have in Jeremiah's day:

"Oh, about $50,000 more than I have now." (Jeremiah would have said shekels.)

"A job in which I can fire other people, but in which I can't be fired."

"Enough 'smarts' to get me out of the scrapes that I seem to get into all the time."

"A burglar-proof padlock on the door and bars on the windows."

Or, if you're asking about getting on the right side of God, you might hear:

"Being a member in good standing of a church."

"Being a member of a Bible-believing church and hearing God's Word preached every Sunday."

"Reading the Bible every day."

But Jeremiah still would say: "That's not good enough." If you really want security, you must understand and know God, the Almighty God of mercy, judgment, and righteousness.

Trusting in the Tangible

One day when Jeremiah finished his sermon, he saw his audience suddenly turn into an angry mob and converge upon him. Quickly he was surrounded. According to Jeremiah 26:8: "The priests and the prophets and all the people took him, saying, 'Thou shalt surely die' "(KJV). He was in danger of being pummeled to death.

What right did this upstart prophet from Anathoth have to tell the priests and the temple prophets what God really required? But what angered them especially was his statement that Jerusalem would become as desolate as Shiloh. It was blasphemy; it was heresy; and besides that, it contradicted what they had been telling the people for years. Jesus received the same kind of intense reaction when He spoke about the temple: "Destroy this temple and in three days I will raise it up"(John 2:19, KJV). They called Him a blasphemer too. Before the mob had a chance to lynch him, the local authorities moved in and arrested him. It was like going from the frying pan into the fire. They hurried him to one of the city gates for a speedy trial. The charge against him was that he had blasphemed the city of God as well as the temple of God. Obviously, he must be a false prophet. As a false prophet, Jeremiah should die. The logic seemed simple enough.

But, of course, the accused should have a chance to defend himself. So they asked Jeremiah to be his own lawyer. For a man who is known as the "weeping prophet," Jeremiah was amazingly cool in his self-defense. It was God who had sent him, he said, "And God told me to tell you to repent or else. However, I realize that I am in your hands right now and you can do to me whatever you wish. If you put me to death, I have to warn you that you will bring innocent blood on your city because I am God's messenger." It was a brief but brilliant defense.

Now the authorities had to deliver their decision. The priests and the official prophets were on one side; a small-town prophet was on the other. In-between were the people who could easily be swayed one way or the other. The authorities had little love for the priests and that might have put them on Jeremiah's side. However, they had less love for prophets. (Not long afterward, another prophet, Urijah, was executed by these same authorities.) So Jeremiah faced an uncertain decision.

One of the telling points of evidence in Jeremiah's favor was the testimony of one of the "elders," probably Ahikam, who had served King Josiah about 15 years earlier when the Book of the Law had been found. He quoted the Prophet Micah who had lived a hundred years earlier in the time of King Hezekiah. Micah had prophesied much the same thing as Jeremiah, and Micah was judged to be a true prophet. King Hezekiah certainly didn't put him to death. Why then should Jeremiah be accused of a capital crime?

The verdict from the princes came back, "Not guilty." Once

again, Jeremiah had escaped near-death. But how would he respond if God called him to go back to preach at the temple again the next day?

We all have our security blankets. The psalmist said, "Some trust in chariots and some in horses"(Ps. 20:7, KJV). Nations trust in armaments; people trust in padlocks, handguns, and karate lessons; and we like to hang onto something tangible like temples and churches.

We own a half dozen Bibles, though on many days not one of them is opened. We call ourselves Bible-believing, but Jeremiah would quickly ask us if we were Bible-practicing. We claim salvation on the basis of a past experience, rather than on the basis of a present reality. We rest in the smug security of our own goodness, a goodness that is predicated on the notion that the sins that we commit are not as vile as those committed by others.

Probably if Jeremiah would come to the front door of our church and preach as he did at the door of the Jerusalem temple, he would be denounced as a false prophet, a heretic, and a rank liberal. Doesn't he know that we are the Lord's people? How dare he upset our security! How dare he say that we are more concerned about going through the motions of our Christianity than we are of practicing it.

Not long ago the Gallup Poll surveyed America's religious involvement. About 81 percent of Americans claim to be religious; 95 percent believe in God; nearly every home has a Bible; nearly half the people can be found in a church or synagogue on a typical weekend; and 92 percent claim a church affiliation. Sounds good, doesn't it?

However, Gallup went on to say that only one in five affirm that religion is the most influential factor of his or her life. And when Gallup began to summarize his findings, he concluded that with only one in eight does religion seem to make a significant difference in the way they actually live their lives. But the most fascinating part of Gallup's survey was the finding that those who are deeply committed to God were happier, had better family relationships, were more tolerant of people from other races and religions, and were more involved in helping the poor, the infirm, and the elderly. No doubt, if Jeremiah had commissioned a Gallup Poll in 609 B.C. he would have discovered the same thing.

6

Clay, Tin Cans, and Silly Putty

Jeremiah 18–19

In *A Diary of Private Prayer,* John Baillie writes, "When the way seems dark before me, give me grace to walk trustingly: When much is obscure to me, let me be all the more faithful to the little that I can clearly see: When the distant scene is clouded, let me rejoice that at least the next step is plain: When what Thou art is most hidden from my eyes, let me still hold fast to what Thou dost command: When insight falters, let obedience stand firm: What I lack in faith, let me repay in love"(Oxford University Press, p. 115).

I wouldn't be surprised if Jeremiah was praying a prayer like that as he hurried away from his trial at the city gate. I can almost picture him, walking quickly at first through the mob, being jostled a bit by some of the ruder sorts and being taunted by others. Then as he turned onto one of the narrow streets of the city, his pace probably slowed.

He had nowhere to go but home . . . nothing to look forward to but tomorrow . . . no friends with whom to share . . . no relatives with whom to relax. Certainly he must have been praising God for deliverance—an almost miraculous deliverance—from the hands of the unruly throng. Yet at the same time he must have been wondering about tomorrow. What would it bring? Where would God send him next?

Would God require him to return to the temple?

If God did, Jeremiah knew that he couldn't do anything but obey, though he probably felt that it would be easier to die in the service of the Lord than to live in the service of the Lord. Sometimes it is easier to be a dead martyr than a living one.

A Visit with the Potter

While the Book of Jeremiah defies chronological arrangement, it seems that Jeremiah's next order from God required him to go just outside the city limits south of the walls of Jerusalem. The story picks up in chapter 18.

You get the feeling that Jeremiah was on call like a substitute school teacher. Sometimes he might be asked to stay in the same school for a week, but at other times he would get an emergency call asking him to show up in a school 20 miles away. And Jeremiah's classes were filled with ruffians.

But this particular morning, God called Jeremiah into an unusual classroom. It was the shop of a potter. No doubt God had two reasons to direct Jeremiah to the potter's house. One was for teacher-training. A good teacher needs to know how to use visual aids. Obviously, Jeremiah's pupils were not getting the message through the lecture technique. A new teaching method might drive home the point. The second reason for Jeremiah to go to the potter's shop was for a lesson that he himself had to learn.

Just outside the city walls, south of the city, was the Valley of Hinnom. Besides being the city dump, the Valley of Hinnom was also the headquarters of the pottery industry. It possessed what the potters needed—a water supply and the right kind of clay.

On this particular day, Jeremiah must have watched silently as the potter's hands worked the clay, removing air pockets, gradually shaping the clump into a useful vessel. Then, just before the vessel was ready for firing in the oven, Jeremiah saw the potter suddenly and forcefully bring his hands together over the vessel, squeezing it again into a formless mass.

The suddenness of the potter's action, the boldness of it—
when the pottery looked good enough to the untrained eye—
was shocking for the moment, but Jeremiah knew what was
happening. The potter had detected a flaw—a serious flaw—
and the pottery would have to be destroyed. The interesting
thing is that the clay wasn't thrown away. Instead, the potter
began molding and shaping that same lump, and soon a new
vessel emerged, more beautiful and more valuable than before.

Lessons? Probably Jeremiah could see some of them himself, but God pointed out a few to him just in case he didn't get
the whole picture. The Divine Potter is sovereign over His
lumps of clay. He can do what He wants to do with them.

Perhaps the surprising thing is that He doesn't throw His
stubborn clay away. Once He has been molding and shaping
it, He keeps working on it. At times, He may have to start from
scratch with it, but He doesn't throw it away.

Of course, the Divine Potter has a dream in His mind—a
vision—for each lump of clay. It may look without form and
void as the earth did in Genesis 1, but God has dreams of
beauty which He intends to bring forth from it, unlikely though
the clay may appear.

The bumper sticker that says, "Be patient; God isn't finished with me yet," could be attached to each lump of clay.
Each one is "in process." "He who began a good work in you
will carry it on to completion until the day of Jesus Christ"
(Phil. 1:6).

F.B. Meyer points out that the potter achieves his purposes
by means of his wheel. The wheel, he says, speaks of the
rounds of life, those routines that often seem so dull and
boring. Round and round the wheel goes, and it is hard to tell
from one revolution to the next if there is any change in the
appearance of the lump of clay. But there is. It may seem
infinitessimal, but with each circuit the molding continues until
the deft hands of the potter feel the process is complete.

Oh, yes, the hands of the potter. The wheel in itself does
nothing. Indeed the wheel is a bore. But the consolation is that

the potter's hands are at work. In His hands, there is not only security—even when He smashes us—but also purpose. Apart from His hands, there is neither security nor purpose.

God likes to remake people. He likes to take Jacobs and Peters and Moseses and Marks and conform them to the image of His Son. The old gospel song uses the image of the Potter as its theme:

Have Thine own way, Lord; have Thine own way.
Thou art the Potter; I am the clay.
Mold me and make me after Thy will,
While I am waiting, yielded and still.

It is sort of ludicrous to think of clay as anything but "yielded and still." But human clay is different. Seldom are we content and still while we are in the process of being molded. We prefer to act like silly putty.

Specifically, however, the message that Jeremiah received at the potter's house was that the nation of Judah was a lump of clay in God's hands, and that God was "preparing" a disaster against them. The word for *preparing* that is used here means "to shape." It was a word that the potters used all the time. The message was clear. If the people did not repent, destruction was coming.

The biggest little word in the English language is the word *if*. God uses it repeatedly in Scripture. In 2 Chronicles 7:14, He says, "If My people . . . will turn from their wicked ways, then will I . . . forgive their sin." While we certainly are clay (and here the analogy fails), we are called to respond to God's "If . . . then" invitations.

Clay has no choice in the matter; we do. It's the old "divine sovereignty—human free-will" debate. The Bible does not teach "either-or" on the subject; it teaches "both-and." So here in the midst of a teaching on God's sovereignty is an invitation requiring man's free response.

Jeremiah's Stern Words

Apparently, when Jeremiah returned to the city and gave this object lesson to the people of Jerusalem, the response wasn't "sackcloth and ashes." Far from it. Of course, Jeremiah was getting accustomed to rejection by this time. What must have surprised him, however, was the different strategy on the part of his antagonists. Realizing that they couldn't count on the authorities to eliminate Jeremiah, they decided to do the job themselves. And they decided to do it with verbal abuse, not physical abuse.

Twice before, in Anathoth and in Jerusalem, Jeremiah's enemies had plotted against his life and had failed. This time they plotted against his reputation with better success.

"Nobody will miss him," they said. After all, the people still had plenty of prophets, priests, and elders milling around the city streets; why did they need Jeremiah?

So a campaign of lies and gossip was launched against God's man. False charges and slander were flung at him. And from the vehemence of Jeremiah's response to it, we can surmise that the attack was quite effective. Jeremiah could withstand physical persecution better than he could take this.

Then, toward the end of chapter 18, the prophet unleashes his bitterest tirade against the people. It was boiling inside of him like a volcano and it had to erupt. Some commentators have been shocked at the fury of Jeremiah's explosion. But it's understandable for two reasons: one is divine, and the other is quite human.

For nearly 20 years, Jeremiah had been God's mouthpiece. He had pleaded, he had prayed, he had wept for these people. When they rejected him, they were rejecting God's messenger, and this hurt Jeremiah most severely. He could take physical persecution better than the rumors and innuendos. In a sense, Jeremiah in his brash imprecation is seeking to view things from God's perspective.

But that may be too noble, and too rational, for what actually was taking place. Jeremiah is very human, in his emotions as well as in his understanding. No matter how godly he was, it would seem that this time he was acting from a human perspective.

He prayed that their children be given to "over to famine,

their wives be made childless and widows, and their young men slain by the sword in battle." He prayed, "Do not forgive their crimes or blot out their sins from Your sight" (Jer. 18:21-23).

As a lump of clay, Jeremiah himself was still in process. God wasn't finished with him yet. Christ's fuller revelation was something Jeremiah didn't have as yet. Christ told us to love our enemies, to forgive them seventy times seven, to feed them and clothe them. Paul reminds us that vengeance belongs to God, not man (Rom. 12:19).

But let's not be too hard on the prophet. Through Jeremiah, God had warned the nation of Judah. Day after day, the prophet had preached that judgment was coming unless they repented. Sometimes he even spelled out the judgments quite graphically. Jeremiah had just come from the potter's house where God once again had said that He was "shaping" a disaster unless His people repented.

Then, when Jeremiah went back in the city and began preaching again, the people laughed at him and lied about him. What more could he do? If the people won't even listen, what's the use? Lower the boom, Lord.

It's easy to identify our position with God's, especially when we have lived with it and struggled to defend it for years. We may have debated our views with friends and neighbors until they became enemies and strangers. And the longer we have held our views, the more we are convinced that they are God's views—so convinced that when someone laughs at us, we are sure that they are laughing at God. Yes, it can happen.

Stern words are certainly called for when we are preaching, teaching, exhorting, and even counseling. But when we are praying, we had best follow the example of our Lord, who warned the people in the strongest terms, but prayed tenderly, "Father, forgive them" (Luke 23:34).

The Broken Jar

Shortly after this episode—it may even have been the next morning for all we know—the Lord told Jeremiah to return to the Hinnom Valley (chap. 19). This time, however, he was not to go alone. On his way out of the city, he was to buy a clay jar, probably from one of the pottery shops just inside the city gate. The word for clay jar that is used here indicates that it was to be a rather small but expensive water jar (probably about 10 inches tall).

Besides buying the jar, Jeremiah was also supposed to round up some of the city elders and priests to accompany him on an unusual field trip. To collect his fellow travelers may have been a bit difficult, especially because these people were not exactly on speaking terms with Jeremiah, and it would be even more difficult when they saw the section of the Valley of Hinnom to which the prophet was leading them.

The Valley of Hinnom stretched across the southern outskirts of the city and curled up on its eastern side as well. Not only was it the headquarters of the pottery industry and the site of the city dump with rubbish burning constantly, but it was also a cemetery of sorts. Here the bodies of criminals, outcasts, and animals were discarded. Sometimes the bodies were buried, and sometimes they were simply left to rot.

But there was something more shocking than that going on in the Valley of Hinnom. The valley was also a shrine for pagan worship, particularly where the god Molech was worshiped. In Molech worship, infants were sacrificed. Molech worship had been suppressed during the time of King Josiah. But now King Jehoiakim was on the throne, and it was again a time of "anything goes" in religion. "Anything" included Molech worship.

So obviously, the somber parade led by Jeremiah, followed by the priests and elders and perhaps a few curious onlookers moved toward that unseemly spot in Jerusalem's landscape. When Jeremiah brought his company to a place overlooking the dreary valley, he stopped, slowly turned around, and delivered the divine message to his captive audience. "Because the people have forsaken Me, says the Lord, and have turned to foreign gods, because they have burned their babies and because they have broken My law over and over and over again, therefore I will break them," and at that moment Jeremiah smashed his expensive jar. "Thus the Lord will break you and your city."

The sound of the breaking of the clay jar must have reverberated dramatically across the entire valley. But it was the symbolism that sent the shock waves even further. When a person wanted to renounce his friendship and bring a curse upon a neighbor, he would stand in front of the neighbor's house and break a jar. Irrevocably, the human relationship was to be broken.

And here was Jeremiah standing just outside the city of Jerusalem, speaking in the name of Jehovah, symbolically breaking a clay jar and renouncing a relationship. The priests and the elders could not have missed the point.

The last time Jeremiah had visited the Valley of Hinnom he had gone to the potter's house and learned the lesson about God's patience and perseverance. This time, Jeremiah buys a clay jar, already formed and set, and breaks it. Now he was demonstrating the judgment of God—just as real, just as important a truth to be reckoned with as God's patience and perseverance. But what were God and Jeremiah so upset about?

1. *People who led double lives.* They worshiped in the temple as if they were true followers of Jehovah, but during the week they worshiped everything else.

2. *The cheapening of human life.* Nowhere on the Jewish landscape was this portrayed more graphically than in the Valley of Hinnom. There, babies were sacrificed at the altars of Molech. There, bodies of criminals and outcasts were discarded to become food for the ravens (see 2 Kings 21:16).

3. *The people's fascination with astrology.* On the rooftops, burnt offerings were presented to astral deities (Jer. 19:13). It was a primitive form of astrology, and many residents of Jerusalem were dabbling in this form of the occult.

4. *The complacence of both religious and civil leaders to immorality and idolatry.* It had begun to sprout again like dandelions on a spring lawn, but the "official" prophets and

priests had closed their eyes to what was going on in the Valley of Hinnom. In order to let them see it, Jeremiah had to take them on a field trip.

If God was upset with His people 2,500 years ago, you can imagine that He might be a little upset about what is going on today. Obviously, the problems of Jeremiah's time are not very different from our own. How easily we look the other way, or pretend we don't see what is going on all around us. It is often easier to contemporize with evil rather than to confront it.

No More Hope

When Jeremiah arrived back in Jerusalem, word must have already arrived about what had transpired in the Valley of Hinnom. Crowds of people were at the temple and Jeremiah didn't have to break another bottle to get their attention. He needed only to reiterate the moral of the object lesson. God was going to bring a disaster upon Jerusalem.

Jeremiah wasn't the last biblical writer to refer to pots and pans. In probably the last epistle he wrote, the Apostle Paul said, "In a large house there are [pots and pans] not only of gold and silver, but also of wood and clay; some are for noble purposes and some for ignoble. If a man cleanses himself from the latter, he will be an instrument for noble purposes, made holy, useful to the Master and prepared to do any good work" (2 Tim. 2:20-21).

Jeremiah could look across the Valley of Hinnom and see the nation he loved as just another tin can in the city dump, another broken jar, shattered and smashed on the valley floor. A jar shaped lovingly and skillfully by the Master Potter, hardened in His oven, painted, decorated artistically to give it beauty, delivered from a shop to a wealthy home for noble use—and then smashed.

How many lives go just like that? And who will pick up the pieces?

God can.

You might think that it is only when the clay is still pliable that the Master Potter can remold and remake. Probably, at this point in his life, that's what Jeremiah thought too. And that was why he was so discouraged.

Jeremiah was rapidly approaching the lowest point in his ministry. The Northern Kingdom of Israel had already been destroyed by the Assyrians. Only the Southern Kingdom remained, with its capital city of Jerusalem and with its valued temple.

But now the prophet had broken the jar. And now it was only a matter of time before Judah, Jerusalem, and the temple would be destroyed. Hope was gone. Perhaps Jeremiah felt as if he should have been left half buried in the trash and broken jars on Hinnom's valley floor.

But at this point there were two things that even Jeremiah couldn't see. First, he didn't see that after 70 years, his people would be returned from captivity. Later, God would reveal that to him, but not yet. So he despaired, even as we do when we cannot see what God can see around the corner.

If we could see beyond today
As God can see,
If all the clouds should roll away,
The shadows flee;
O'er present griefs we would not fret,
Each sorrow we would soon forget,
For many joys are waiting yet,
For you and me.

If we could know beyond today,
As God doth know,
Why dearest treasures pass away,
And tears must flow,
And why the darkness leads to light,
Why dreary days will soon grow bright;
Some day life's wrongs will be made right—
Faith tells us so.

—Norman Clayton

Jeremiah didn't know it yet, but God was preparing a friend for him. In the closing verses of chapter 19, you see a change in writing style. Jeremiah is described in the third person, not as the person telling the story. Someone else has come onto the scene.

At times, you may think life is impossible. At times, you may not be able to imagine that anything good is happening, or even that anything good can possibly happen. You have examined all the alternatives and all the alternatives are bad. That's the way Jeremiah felt at the close of chapter 19. But he was wrong. Something good *was* happening—even in the valley of clay, silly putty, broken jars, and smashed tin cans.

Yes, God knows how to pick up the pieces. He can not only mold the soft clay in the potter's shop, but He can also put together the brittle pieces.

God is still at work. Never forget it.

7

The Fine Art of Dust-Dwelling

Jeremiah 20; 35

F.B. Meyer, that great British Bible teacher from the turn of the century, preached a classic sermon entitled "Are You Dwelling in the Dust?" His text was a little known verse in Isaiah: "Awake and sing, ye that dwell in dust, for thy dew is as the dew of herbs" (Isa. 26:19).

He began his sermon like this:

> In earlier days, you may have been very conscious of the clear shining of God's face. You awoke in the morning and God was there. . . . That was your lot once. . . . You felt you were Christ's companion; that He was using you, and that there was a constant interchange of holy fellowship between Him and you. But for some reason which you cannot understand, the morning light has died out of your life, and instead of your sitting with Christ upon the throne, in the constant enjoyment of fellowship with Him, you have been brought down into the very dust of neglect and forsakenness: and for a long time now you have been saying, "My God, my God, why hast Thou forsaken me?" You cannot imagine why.

By the time F.B. Meyer was five minutes into his message he

had pinpointed five different kinds of people who could be dwelling in the dust: (1) Those who feel themselves forsaken of God; (2) those who have lost the power of locating Christ in prayer; (3) those whose ideals are behind them and withered; (4) those who are passing through difficult physical or financial times; and (5) those who are caught in a job or a situation that they cannot reverse.

Everyone has been in one of those situations at least once in his or her life, and probably more than once. But Jeremiah—poor Jeremiah—seemed to be bogged down in all five of those situations simultaneously. No wonder he was depressed. He may have been playing with the clay of Hinnom in chapters 18 and 19, but when he gets into chapter 20, he is dwelling in the dust.

In the Stocks

We ended the last chapter in the middle of a story. Jeremiah had taken elders of the people and elders of the priests into the Valley of Hinnom and had broken his expensive jar in a dramatic gesture, signifying that God would break Jerusalem in the same way. Just as Hinnom had become a trash pile, a garbage dump, so God would make the entire city of Jerusalem a trash pile.

When Jeremiah returned to the temple and preached the same message, he wasn't exactly greeted with thunderous applause. The people *did* listen to him; that seemed like an improvement on the status quo. But what Jeremiah was saying verged on treason. The year was probably 606 B.C. Nebuchadnezzar of Babylon was making his drive against Egypt to establish world dominance and little Judah was in the way. To say that Jerusalem would become a trash heap was morale-shattering at best, and certainly could very easily be construed as treasonous.

So Pashur, the chief of the temple police, decided his police force should take care of Jeremiah. Rather than let Jeremiah get the people shaken up by his prophetic ravings, Pashur ordered the prophet to be beaten. No doubt, Jeremiah received the full 40 lashes allowed under Mosaic Law (Deut. 25:3). Then to make sure that Jeremiah got the message and to make sure that the people didn't take Jeremiah seriously again, Pashur placed the prophet in the stocks, a torture device used specifically for false prophets (2 Chron. 16:10; Jer. 29:26).

The word for *stocks* comes from a Hebrew word for distort. It didn't take Jeremiah long to understand why. His feet, hands, and neck were held fast and his contorted body was almost doubled up. Spending an entire night in such a twisted position after a brutal whiplashing was inhumane physical punishment. But perhaps the deepest cut of all was the fact that Jeremiah was consigned to the punishment for false prophets.

The location was the northern gate of the upper temple court, one of the most conspicuous places in the city. Late at night and early in the morning the area was swarming with people, laughing at the helpless prophet. It was a cruel laughter—something like the jeers that Jesus faced on the cross: "He saved others; Himself He cannot save" (Matt. 27:42). To Jeremiah, they might have mocked, "He predicted terror for others; let's put a little terror into him."

When morning came, so did Pashur, the overseer. Pashur had succeeded in not only making Jeremiah a laughingstock, but also in labeling him a false prophet. And before the civil authorities could come and say that Pashur had exceeded his authority, he released him.

Pashur was through with Jeremiah, but Jeremiah wasn't through with Pashur. Jeremiah had a parting shot. "From now on," Jeremiah said, "the Lord calls you not Pashur, but 'Terror-all-around.'" It was a phrase that Jeremiah had used before to capsulize what was coming to his nation (see Jer. 6:25).

Besides giving Pashur a new name, Jeremiah also identifies the nation's new nemesis for the first time. Previously, he had referred to the enemy from the north. Now "the enemy from the north" is definitely identified as Babylon. Pashur himself, along with his family would be taken into captivity, Jeremiah predicted, and he would die there. That would prove who the real false prophet was. At this point it may not have taken too much foresight to identify the Babylonians as the enemy from the north. They were coming on strong and had already defeated the Assyrians. But to identify Pashur as one of those to be taken captive was so personally specific that it must have shaken all those who heard it.

Evidently, within the next decade, Pashur was indeed taken captive, for the next we hear about the position of the temple's chief of police (29:24-28), someone else is holding the post and he has just received a letter from exiled priests held captive in Babylon.

You Deceived Me!

As Jeremiah went home, joy bells weren't ringing in his heart. He was discouraged. He was also shockingly honest before God. His cry begins, "O Lord, You deceived me," and ends, "Why did I ever come out of the womb?" (20:7-18)

These are hardly the expressions of overcoming faith, love, and joy that you would expect from a major prophet. But commentator A.S. Peake calls these verses "one of the most powerful and impressive passages in the whole of the prophetic literature, a passage which takes us, as no other, not only into the depths of the prophet's soul, but into the secrets of the prophetic consciousness."

One of the puzzling elements of this passage is a verse of joy right in the middle. "Sing to the Lord; praise the Lord! For He has delivered the life of the needy from the hand of evildoers" (v. 13, RSV). Then after that single verse of joy, Jeremiah returns immediately to, "Cursed be the day on which I was born!" (v. 21, RSV)

Some scholars feel that the verse of joy separates two parts of Jeremiah's frank confession—that he tried to be joyful, but his joy lasted only for a minute before he reverted to despair. Others agree that there are two distinct parts to this confession, but they feel that these two parts may have been uttered at two very separate times. Still others feel that the verses probably got out of order in the past 2,000 years. They suggest that verses 14 through 18 should be placed before verses 7 through 13, not afterward. One such evangelical scholar suggests it is much more logical to think of the verses as being transposed, while another one says, "Jeremiah was never known for smooth transitions." Neither view can be proven.

While there's doubt about how the verses fit together, there's no doubt at all about Jeremiah's mood. He was at the bottom. He had experienced "down" periods repeatedly during his 20 year prophetic ministry, but this was the nadir. He had no friends, no followers, no converts. He had been run out of his hometown and evicted from the temple. The enemy was on its way, and Jeremiah somehow felt as if he had been the agent of his own nation's destruction. Though he had been faithful in delivering God's message, it had been a message of destruction—the destruction of everything that was nearest and dearest to him.

So somehow, Jeremiah had the notion (which he probably had absorbed from the populace at large) that if he weren't around, destruction wouldn't come. He was not only the messenger; he felt he was also the message. The medium had become the message.

No wonder he cursed the day he was born. He didn't curse God, nor did he curse his parents, but he wished that he had never seen the light of day. Wouldn't the world have been better off if he had never been born? Besides, what had he accomplished anyway, except to pave the way for the total destruction of the nation and people he loved?

"Lord, You deceived me" (v. 7). Jeremiah wasn't accusing God of lying, but rather of luring him into becoming a prophet. In legal terms, Jeremiah felt God was guilty of entrapment. He had put Jeremiah into a position where he didn't have any choice, and now Jeremiah had to bear the brunt of everything.

Jeremiah's message was one of destruction and terror, so that he had been known by the same nickname that he had given to Pashur, "Terror-on-every-side." As a sensitive man, that was a message Jeremiah didn't enjoy preaching. He was tempted to turn in his "prophet's card" and look for another job, but he was trapped. He was helpless. As he puts it, God's Word was like a fire in his bones (v. 9). He couldn't keep it within himself, even if he resolved to do so.

God had given him a sensitive nature; why then had God also given him a job that seemed to require insensitivity? God had given him a warm heart, a heart that could easily be broken; why then had God called him to do something that seemed to require a callous heart?

The inner conflict was almost too much for Jeremiah to bear, and so his feelings bubbled to the surface, even when he was down in the depths. One commentator says it was Jeremiah's ability to vent his feelings to God that may have saved his sanity: "On account of his deep faith in God, and because he did not hesitate to give vent to his feelings of despair and bitterness, the tension of his inner life did not cause him to break down." Blessed is the man who has a God he can trust with his feelings.

Divine Promises

Despite Jeremiah's depression, he kept returning to some divine promises. God is faithful and will keep His Word. When Jeremiah was called to be a prophet, God had promised to be with him and deliver him (1:8). So even in his despair he could say, "The Lord is with me like a mighty warrior" (20:11).

Jeremiah knew also that God was just and righteous. Everything seemed confused and impossible to sort out, but God could sort it out. God examines men's hearts, and in the end accomplishes His purposes.

At times, Jeremiah viewed God almost as an adversary, and yet God was the only true friend he had. This was Jeremiah's confusion, but it was also his consolation.

It is because of Jeremiah's knowledge of God that he can still see a crack of light in the darkness. Nothing else emits a glimmer. Apart from God there is no hope; as long as Jeremiah keeps his eyes on himself and on his fellow man, the world seems hopeless. The clouds are dark and heavy; the sun seems to have disappeared. But Jeremiah knows that somewhere above the clouds, the sun is still shining even though he cannot see it.

John Oxenham once wrote:
> Never once since the world began
> Has the sun ever stopped his shining.
> His face very often we could not see,
> And we grumbled at his inconstancy;
> But the clouds were really to blame, not he,
> For, behind them, he was shining.
>
> And so—behind life's darkest clouds
> God's love is always shining.
> We veil it at times with our faithless fears,
> And darken our sight with our foolish tears,
> But in time the atmosphere always clears,
> For His love is always shining.

In an old inn, the Chesa Veglia, at St. Moritz in the Swiss Alps is an inscription in German that reads: *Wenn du denkst es geht nicht mehr, kommt von irgendwo ein lichtein her.* When you translate that into English, it says: *When you think everything is hopeless, a little ray of light comes from somewhere.*

No matter how severe the trial, the Christian always has the Holy Spirit's provision to bear him along. Isaiah wrote, "Who is among you that feareth the Lord, that obeyeth the voice of his servant, that walketh in darkness, and hath no light? Let him trust in the name of the Lord, and stay upon his God" (Isa. 50:10, KJV).

That isn't easy. Trusting God in the darkness takes faith, but it is by faith that we are commanded to walk. No, it isn't easy. We much prefer walking in the light. But it was in the darkness that God called Jeremiah to walk before Him.

Job speaks of God, holding back the face of His throne and spreading His cloud upon it (Job 26:9). In a devotional application of that verse, George Matheson, the virtually blind Scot hymn writer and clergyman, wrote, "We can understand a hiding of His beauty, for the beauty of the minor chord may only appear in the symphony. We can understand a hiding of His counsels, for we in our ignorance might not see the good of them. But we should always like to see His sovereignty." And that is what the throne of God symbolizes.

Then Matheson refers to the double act of God's concealment. God not only "holds back the face of His throne," but He also "spreads a cloud over it." Admittedly, these are difficult times for the Christian, but they should not lead us into despair. After all, says Matheson, "It is only the face of the throne. The face of the throne is that which looks forward; it is God's sovereignty seen in advance. He will not reveal that." But, says Matheson, "He will reveal the back of His throne. He will let us see His providence in retrospect.

"Who would not climb the hill of God if it were always crowned with sunshine? If there is too much light there can be no test of love. It is easy for you to seek your God when you see the rainbow of emerald and the blaze of sapphire. But if the rainbow were extinguished, if the sapphire blaze be quenched, if the face of His throne be covered, could you see Him then?"

Jeremiah did. Even in his total darkness.

You may not realize it, but God is nearer to you when you are low than when you are lofty. Of course, the Lord never forsakes us, so in a technical sense He is *always* with us. But it is when we most need His care that He stoops the lowest to help us.

Not only is God very close at such times—whether you *feel* it or not—but you are very close to being something God can use. God did not make us out of rocks, but out of dust. And it is often when we are "sitting in the dust" that God can make the most of us.

What happened to poor, depressed, discouraged Jeremiah? How did God get him out of his deep funk? Apparently, God allowed some other needy people to cross his path—the Rechabites. In some ways, this was a perfect match. No one else had much to do with the Rechabites, and the Rechabites were too new in town to realize that no one else had much to do with Jeremiah.

The Rechabites had been among the few good neighbors that the Israelites ever had. The Children of Israel first bumped into them when both tribes were wandering in the wilderness. The Rechabites were practically the only nomadic tribe to show God's people any kindness.

During the years after Moses, these people began worshiping Jehovah. In the time of Elijah (about 850 B.C.) they, like the intrepid prophet, were dismayed with the corruption in both the Northern and Southern Kingdoms. They took a vow never again to drink wine, nor live in houses, nor plant seed from that time on.

Two hundred years had passed since that promise. For most of the time the Rechabites continued to wander through the wilderness chasing their sheep, goats, camels, and whatever else nomads usually chase.

But now (606 B.C.) as Nebuchadnezzar of Babylon started his drive into the area, the Rechabites felt that they had better flee to Jerusalem for safety. So, much to the consternation of the Jews, the Rechabites pitched their tents in the city streets and kept their animals outside the walls. The Jews, meanwhile, knew that the Rechabites meant no harm. But after all, they were smelly nomads and weren't blood brothers.

It was an awkward situation. The Jews couldn't kick the Rechabites out, but they certainly didn't want to make them feel *too* comfortable. Besides, their presence was another sign that Jeremiah may have been right about the Babylonians.

Then came Jeremiah. He befriended the Rechabites and invited them to enter the temple. Certain side rooms of the temple were available for the use of the Levites, and apparently Jeremiah still had one or two priests that he could talk into letting him use a room.

So Jeremiah escorted the Rechabites into a private room. As they entered, they saw bowls of wine and cups. As a good host, Jeremiah invited them to drink. Though it was a prophet who had given the invitation and though they were in the hallowed temple of the Jews, they refused, adhering to their vow made 250 years earlier.

It was another object lesson for the Children of Israel. Though the Rechabites weren't even true sons of Israel, they remained faithful to their promises to God. On the other hand, the true sons of Israel had forgotten their promises to God, and so disaster would soon overtake them. After Jeremiah finished reminding the Jews of impending disaster, he pronounced a blessing on the Rechabites for their faithfulness to God.

But there was also another object lesson, a personal message for Jeremiah. He had thought of himself as abused, unappreciated, and ineffective. He had wondered why he had been born. He had wondered why God had called him to such an impossible task. Rather than answering him directly, God gave him the example of the Rechabites, who had lived with an impossible vow for 250 years, who had lived a lifestyle out of keeping with the worldly society of Israel, who had been lowly and despised for generation after generation—and yet they remained faithful to Jehovah.

Maybe it's not a complete answer, but God showed that others in even more difficult circumstances than Jeremiah have stood the test, and he could stand it too, if he continued living faithfully before God one day at a time.

Later in life, Jeremiah caught a loftier glimpse of faithfulness. It was the faithfulness of God Himself. In the midst of Jeremiah's somber Lamentations, a book that could easily induce depression all by itself, Jeremiah acknowledges that God's compassions "fail not. They are new every morning. Great is Thy faithfulness" (Lam. 3:22-23, KJV). The *Jerusalem Bible* translates it this way: "The favors of Jehovah are not all past, His kindnesses are not exhausted; every morning they are renewed; great is Thy faithfulness."

Jeremiah was learning the value of experiencing God's renewable daily mercies. There was another thing that Jeremiah was learning. He tells about it in the following verses in Lamentations: "The Lord, I say, is all that I have; therefore I will wait for Him patiently. . . .It is good to wait in patience"(3:24, 26, NEB).

He didn't say, "It is easy." He said, "It is good."

8

Is This the Happiness?

Jeremiah 25; 36; 45

Pilgrim's Progress is not what you would call a book of humor, but there are some lines in it that certainly rate more than a mere chuckle.

I like the line from the lips of Pliable when he and Christian are sloshing through the Slough of Despond. Christian had talked him into joining the pilgrimage, and Pliable has always been a bit skeptical that the two of them will really get anywhere. After considerable time in the Slough of Despond, Christian is starting to wonder too. Then, after all their attempts to get themselves out have only plunged them deeper into it, Pliable looks up at Christian and with a somber face asks, "Is this the happiness you spoke to me of?"

I think of that line whenever I feel frustrated, totally trapped by circumstances over which I have no control. I suppose the experience is common to everyone. I'm sure that you too have felt like Pliable, mired in quicksand, and the harder you try to get out, the deeper you slide into the bog.

The biblical character I associate with such an experience is not Jeremiah, but a cohort of his named Baruch. Baruch was probably a secretary or an official aide to one of the ruling elders of Jerusalem, who was escorted by Jeremiah on the sight-seeing trip through the Valley of Hinnom. At the time Jeremiah probably didn't realize that Baruch's sympathies were with him. But in the next year, Baruch and Jeremiah had joined forces. At least, they had a working agreement.

Baruch Joins the Team

The last chapter—in which Jeremiah hit the bottom of his despair—transpired in about 606 B.C. Now the year is 605 B.C., the fourth year of King Jehoiakim's reign (Jer. 36). At this point there's no question about it—Jeremiah has a teammate named Baruch.

Perhaps Baruch had realized that Jeremiah's oral ministry was hampered because of the opposition of the temple leaders. Perhaps he had volunteered his services to help the prophet extend his ministry by putting his words down in writing. Or perhaps it was Jeremiah who took the initiative, sensing some sympathy on the part of Baruch and then drawing him into his service. We don't know the specifics, but somehow the two got together.

It may have been a tentative move for Baruch, but it was still a courageous one. After all, he was from a noble family, had a good education, and probably had a good job working for one of the city's officials, a job that would be a stepping-stone to bigger and better things in the future. We know that his grandfather was the "governor" of Jerusalem in earlier years, and that his brother later rose to prominence in civic affairs. So no doubt Baruch ben Neriah would have enjoyed the same upward nobility.

In 1978, scholars identified "with absolute certainty" two biblical names from the same passage in Scripture. According to an archeologist at Jerusalem's Hebrew University, this is the first time that such a discovery has ever been made. The names were found on seal-inscriptions. The two seals, made of clay, sealed papyrus documents, no doubt housed in the official archives. The names were those of Jerahmeel (Jer. 36:26) and Baruch.

One of the seals says, "Belonging to Baruch, son of Neriah,

the scribe." There is no doubt that this is the same Baruch who became Jeremiah's secretary. The other seal says, "Belonging to Jerahmeel, the king's son," which is exactly how Jerahmeel is referred to in Jeremiah 36:26 (NASB). Also mentioned in the seals is Seraiah (51:59), who is referred to as a brother of Baruch.

These archeological findings substantiate the fact that Baruch gave up a promising governmental position to become Jeremiah's scribe. Interestingly, the name *Baruch* means blessedness or happiness. Can you picture Mr. Happiness going to work for Jeremiah? You can imagine the jokes that must have been passed along the streets of Jerusalem regarding that unlikely combination. If ever there was an odd couple, this was it: "Happy" Baruch and "the weeping prophet" Jeremiah.

On the political front, things were heating up. Nebuchadnezzar's Babylonian troops had defeated the Egyptian forces in the historic battle of Carchemish on the Euphrates River. To secure his hold on trade routes in and out of Egypt, Nebuchadnezzar had begun a systematic decimation of all the smaller nations and cities along the way. That would inevitably include Judah and its capital Jerusalem. Probably in 606 B.C. Nebuchadnezzar had visited Jerusalem. When he left after this "friendly" visit, he took with him some of the brightest and best of Jerusalem's youth, including a young man named Daniel (Dan. 1:1-6).

Chapters 25, 36, and 45 of Jeremiah take place in the next two years. First, in chapter 25, Jeremiah gives his people one last chance. "You have not listened," he tells the people four times (vv. 3-4, 7-8). "And because you have not listened, your land will become a 'desolate wasteland' and you will serve Babylon for 70 years" (see v. 11).

Much of this message had been preached in slightly different ways before, but two ideas were novel. One was that Judah's captivity would last for 70 years.

(Scholars have debated about how literally we should understand the 70 years. A case can be made for a literal 70-year period, but most conservative scholars today feel that it could just as well have meant a rounded number, indicating the normal lifetime of a person. Nebuchadnezzar deported the residents in three stages: 605 B.C., 598 B.C., and 586 B.C., and the ending of the Captivity is also dated in various ways from 538 B.C., and 536 B.C. when the resettlement of Jerusalem began, to 516 B.C. when Zerubbabel's temple was completed.)

The other novel idea was the naming of Nebuchadnezzar as God's servant. That was more than any good patriotic Jew could stomach. It was like calling Hitler or Stalin God's servant.

Scripture doesn't spell out the reaction of the authorities to Jeremiah's latest outburst, but a little imagination can fill in the details. As we begin chapter 36, we find that Jeremiah is "confined." Probably Jeremiah had been warned that if he set foot in the temple courtyard again, he would be immediately arrested and taken to the king where his fate would be decided. The king did not care for prophets in general, nor for Jeremiah in particular, so a trial before the king would lead to a foregone conclusion.

Temporarily, Jeremiah may have been stymied, but only temporarily. He knew, however, that if he couldn't proclaim the message orally, God would want him to get the message out some other way. That's when Baruch comes on the scene.

Second Thoughts

The year is 605 B.C. The prophet is told by God to put all his words into writing. Obeying God's command, he summoned Baruch and began dictating message after message. Day in, day out, Baruch wrote; week in, week out, he wrote. Since Jeremiah had been preaching and prophesying for about 22 years, it took both time and effort to condense all of this onto one lengthy scroll.

It wasn't the ideal job. Working conditions? Not too good. Possibility for advancement? Nil. Fringe benefits? None. Pension? No need to think about the future with Nebuchadnezzar scheduled for a return engagement any month.

But Baruch did his work. As a professional scribe, he knew his task well. When he finished the scroll, he no doubt rolled it up carefully, tied and sealed it neatly, and then handed it with care to Jeremiah.

Much to Baruch's surprise, Jeremiah handed the scroll back to him. Then he explained in words something like this: "I have been forbidden to preach in the temple, and even if I could preach, no one would listen. They laugh at me, you know. They call me 'Terror-all-around.' You know that it would do no good for me to preach in the temple even if I could, don't you, Baruch?"

Baruch must have nodded slowly, but he probably did not fully comprehend where the conversation was heading.

"That's why I want you to take my place, Baruch. I want you to go to the temple. I want you to open the scroll and read God's Word to the people. After all, you are from a prominent Jerusalem family. Maybe they will listen to you; maybe they will repent if they hear God's Word from your lips."

Baruch must have gulped a big gulp. This wasn't in his job description. Indeed, this wasn't even one of his spiritual gifts. He was a writer, not a preacher; a scribe, not a prophet.

But something else must have bothered him. It was one thing to be associated with Jeremiah in the privacy of his own apartment; it was another thing to be Jeremiah's spokesman in the temple courtyard. Baruch's old friends would be there, his social peers—the people he would need to impress if he was going to go back to his former life. His career would be ruined if he went to the temple courtyard and preached Jeremiah's words. It would mean no turning back.

Chronologically, chapter 45 of Jeremiah fits in here, between verses 7 and 8 of chapter 36. It is here that Baruch says something similar to what Pliable said in the Slough of Despond: "Is this the happiness you spoke to me of?" Actually, his words came out more like: "Woe is me, Lord, for You have added insult to injury." Or to be more precise, in King James English, "Woe is me now! For the Lord hath added grief to my sorrow" (45:3).

It doesn't sound like Mr. Happiness speaking, does it? But can you blame him? He had already made a tremendous personal sacrifice when he began working for Jeremiah. Of course, he sympathized with Jeremiah, and of course he mourned about his nation's insensitivity to their sin. But he still had some hopes and dreams for a personal future.

Now all his plans were in jeopardy. If he went out in that temple courtyard with Jeremiah's scroll, it would mean the end of everything for Baruch. He might be laughed at, as Jeremiah was. He might be arrested, as Jeremiah would have been. He might also be beaten, as Jeremiah would have been. And quite possibly, he might be mobbed and lynched and sentenced to death as a traitor, a turncoat, or a Babylonian spy, as Jeremiah would have been.

Besides the physical and psychological suffering, Baruch was being asked by God to do something that he really couldn't do. At least, that was what he thought. Baruch was a good man, a noble man, and a righteous man, but Baruch was still looking out for Number One.

Good works and righteous deeds can easily be tinged with selfishness. Motives are frequently mixed. Sometimes only God can sort them out, but it is helpful to face up honestly to the human mixture that accounts for so much of our religious activity.

Why do you go to church? Your first two reasons will probably be pious ones, but then you might find some very personal and selfish reasons cluttering up the remainder. Why do you read your Bible? Why do you visit the sick? Why do you send greeting cards?

And why, Baruch, were you willing to go to work for Jeremiah anyway—if you weren't willing to sacrifice everything for him?

God's Answer to Baruch

Chapter 45 is the shortest chapter in the entire Book of Jeremiah, but it is written entirely and expressly for Baruch. In it, God gives Baruch a threefold answer.

1. God says to Baruch: "If you want to compare unhappiness, what is your unhappiness compared to Mine? If you want to compare hurts, what is your hurt compared to Mine? These are My chosen people. I have given them all they could ask for. I love them, but they have rejected Me. And are you complaining about your hurt?"

Before you feel your pain, God feels it. The New Testament tells us that we do not have a God who cannot be touched by the feeling of our infirmities (Heb. 4:15). The sword that pricks your skin has already wounded Him.

2. God says to Baruch: "This is no time for personal ambition. If you are interested in serving Me, it must be on My terms, not yours."

We live in an age of "Looking Out for Number One." In such an age, Jeremiah 45:5 is a text that should be engraved on the heart of every Christian worker: "Are you seeking great things for yourself? Seek them not" (RSV).

In 1801, England's prestigious Cambridge University tested its mathematics students to rank them properly in their class. Cambridge did this every year, so there was nothing unusual about the taking of the exam. What was unusual was a young man who had recently given himself to the Lord for His service. He was a good student, but sometimes at exam time the tension completely overwhelmed him. Recently he had failed two tests, and now the competition was so intense that he didn't have much hope of faring any better. As the date of the exam drew closer, it became all he could think about; his mind was increasingly confused.

Just at that time, he recalled a sermon he had heard only a few weeks earlier. The text: Jeremiah 45:5. "Seekest thou great things for thyself? Seek them not" (KJV). Henry Martyn went on, not only to win the top ranking in his class, but also to become a pioneer missionary to Persia and India, accomplishing much for the glory of God.

Regarding his winning the top award at Cambridge, he later remarked, "I obtained my highest wishes, but was surprised to find I had grasped a shadow."

We don't know what great things Baruch ben Neriah was seeking, but doubtless they too would have shriveled into shadows if he had attained them. He might have wished to become governor of Jerusalem, a position his grandfather had held. He might have thought of the great things he could have done for the Lord, if he held that post, seemingly greater things than he could accomplish serving as a scribe for a weeping prophet.

But God knows better than we do where the greatest things are, and where are the matters that have eternal importance.

In a little poem called "Submission," George Herbert summarizes it well:

How know I, if Thou shouldst me raise,
That I should then raise Thee?
Perhaps great places and Thy praise
Do not so well agree.

Alexander Stewart in his warm exposition of Jeremiah cites another notable figure whose life was turned around by this verse. The man was John R. Mott. As a student at Cornell University and the son of a prosperous business leader, John Mott anticipated a career in law and politics if not in business. But one day he decided to attend a religious meeting at the university. Arriving a bit late, he slipped into the meeting and was taking his seat just as the speaker began with the words: "Seekest thou great things for thyself? Seek them not." And then the speaker added from the Sermon on the Mount: "But seek ye first the kingdom of God" (Matt. 6:33, KJV).

Mott heard and remembered little else from the speaker that day, but those three short sentences revolutionized his life. He went on to become not a wealthy businessman nor an influential politician, but rather a leader in recruiting young men and women for world-wide missionary service.

John Oxenham once wrote:

Is thy place a small place?
Tend it with care;
He set you there.

It was a lesson for Baruch to learn.

3. God says to Baruch: "I will be with you and will preserve your life." That is the sense of Jeremiah 45:5, a rather difficult verse for translators. Literally it is, "I will give you your life as a prize of war." In other words, God is telling Baruch, "I'm not promising you a rose garden. You are in a war and it won't be easy. However, I will be there with you and your life will be protected."

The nation would be facing catastrophe and even Jeremiah and Baruch would witness the destruction of all their possessions. But God promised them that their lives would be spared.

God doesn't oversell. Moses had given up life in a palace in Egypt to lead his people out of bondage. But when they conversed on Mount Sinai, God didn't promise him a new palace in the Promised Land. Rather, He promised him: "My presence shall go with you, and I will give you rest" (Ex. 33:14).

When Jesus left His disciples, He didn't promise sweetness and light. He told them, "In the world you have tribulation, but be of good cheer, I have overcome the world" (John 16:33, RSV). He also told them of His Holy Spirit who was being sent to them and who would remain with them (vv.7-15).

It was enough for the first-century Christians and it is enough for us today. For Baruch, it meant getting back to work. And work meant taking Jeremiah's place, reading the scroll in the temple.

Into the Fire

The date can be quite precisely fixed—December 604 B.C. A fast had been proclaimed—not by the king, but by the people—and the city of Jerusalem was thronged. News had come that Nebuchadnezzar had sacked the Philistine stronghold of Ashkelon, only about 35 miles away. Naturally, all the residents of Judah were terrified. Perhaps what Jeremiah had predicted would come to pass after all. Were they next on Nebuchadnezzar's list?

Into that anxious and volatile environment, Baruch walked with his scroll. First, Baruch went to a friend's apartment, which was located in the upper courtyard of the temple. Though the friend was not at home, his son, recognizing Baruch, gave permission for the use of the apartment. Perhaps standing in the doorway or else leaning out the window, Baruch summoned his loudest voice and began reading the lengthy scroll. The apartment not only gave him some safety, but also may have provided some amplification for his voice. As he read the scroll at this site near the New Gate, Baruch must have taken note that only a couple years before, Jeremiah was on trial for his life at this very place.

This time, Baruch knew that he was the one who was on the spot. He was doing something that had never been done before—reading publicly the words of a prophet—and Baruch knew that the crowd could erupt with the same hostility that Jeremiah had confronted earlier.

As the son of the apartment owner heard Baruch read the words from the scroll and as he saw the reaction of the crowds, he hurriedly left and ran to find his father, who was in the midst of a cabinet meeting in the king's palace. Bursting in, the son reported to his father what he had heard. Quickly, the cabinet meeting was adjourned. A scribe was sent to get Baruch and bring him and his scroll back to the palace as soon as possible.

Baruch was treated deferentially by the men; apparently he was one of their peers and was certainly not a stranger to them. He was asked to read the scroll, which he did, from beginning to end.

What must have impressed the officials was the accuracy of Jeremiah's earlier prophecies. Now it was all taking place before their eyes. At the beginning of his prophetic ministry, about 22 years earlier, he had warned about the power from the north when there seemed to be no power in the north at all. Now Nebuchadnezzar's forces were breathing on them.

Their first reaction was fear. Then, collecting their thoughts, they realized that this would all have to be reported to the king. In preparing their report, they cross-examined Baruch regarding the scroll and how it came to be written.

Surmising that King Jehoiakim would not appreciate Jeremiah's written message any better than he had appreciated Jeremiah's oral messages, they advised Baruch to take Jeremiah and find a safe hiding place (Jer. 36:19). They knew that the lives of both Jeremiah and Baruch were in utmost danger. You can be sure that Baruch knew it too. A prophet named Urijah had already been slain by the king, and his body had been thrown into the Valley of Hinnom to rot (26:20-23). The officials knew their king would not hesitate to do the same to Jeremiah and Baruch.

While Baruch and Jeremiah were finding a safe hiding place, the officials went to the king and reported what they had heard. At first, the officials attempted to keep the scroll out of the king's hands, but he insisted on seeing it.

One of the cabinet members, a scribe, read the scroll to the king. As he read, the others watched to see the royal response. King Jehoiakim reacted as the officials had feared he would. Since it was December, the king kept a charcoal fire burning in a brazier in the middle of his room. As the scribe finished reading a section of the scroll, the king took a scribe's knife, cut off the strip from the scroll, and tossed it into the fire. Strip by strip, the precious manuscript was incinerated.

Perhaps it was good that Baruch was not present to witness the sacrilege. It would have been more than he could bear.

Jehoiakim's father had trembled when he heard God's Word, but Jehoiakim showed no fear whatever. Instead, he ordered Jeremiah and Baruch arrested.

Where Jeremiah and Baruch went is not known, but this much is sure. They were in a safe place, because the Bible says that the Lord hid them (36:26). And when the Lord hides you, no one will find you.

Baruch and Jeremiah soon received a detailed report of what had transpired in the king's palace. Though Baruch knew very well what kind of a man Jehoiakim was, he still must have been appalled by the king's blatant disregard of God's Word.

Besides that, Baruch must have been nearly grief-stricken.

He had lost something very precious. This was not the day of portable typewriters, word processors, carbon paper, and copy machines. A scroll was a rare possession. A scribe was a craftsman laboring over his work. A completed manuscript was treasured. Of course, Baruch believed that his manuscript should have been specially prized, because it contained the message of God speaking to His people through His Prophet Jeremiah. Now literally, it had gone up in smoke.

The Powerful Overcomer

It was beginning to dawn on Baruch what God was trying to teach him with the words: "Seekest thou great things for thyself? Seek them not."

But another emotion must also have been wracking his system. He was a scribe. That was his training; that was his talent. If God couldn't use his service as a scribe, what good was he to God? King Jehoiakim may have been the one who tore his precious scroll into shreds, but it was God Himself who was cutting Baruch down to size. Baruch must have wondered what he was good for. If God allowed weeks and months of his efforts and finest talents to be wasted, how could God possibly use anything else that he possessed?

Baruch didn't understand what God was doing. Hadn't he taken the first step by offering his services to Jeremiah? Wasn't that an indication of humility? But then Jeremiah had ordered him to read the scroll in the temple courtyard. That meant public humiliation. Then his scroll was ripped to shreds and burned by the king. That meant professional humiliation.

Hiding out, who knows where, with Jeremiah as his moody partner, Baruch must have felt akin to Elijah when we was hiding from Queen Jezebel. Only a year before, Baruch was a noble scribe, looked up to in Jerusalem's finest circles, with a bright and promising future. Now he had been brought low before God, and the one talent which he had thought he possessed had been rendered useless. What else could he give God?

Frequently, God has to bring us low. Not only does He not

want us to be self-seeking, but also He does not want us to be self-serving. Service, even the service of God, can be self-gratifying. We are more interested in becoming self-fulfilled than we are in selfless worship.

We forget that God does not need to use us. As much as that may be a blow to our pride, it is true. He does not need to use us. Nothing we can do can add to His greatness. He alone is self-sufficient. Even Baruch, from a good family, with considerable talents, had to learn, like the Apostle Paul, to count it all loss.

The poet John Milton bemoaned that because of his blindness, "that one talent which is death to hide lodged with me useless, though my soul more bent to serve therewith my Master." And Baruch, another professional writer, must have felt the same way.

But these traumatic experiences must also have reminded Baruch of God's special message to him. Like Christian in *Pilgrim's Progress* in the Castle of the Giant Despair, he must have found the key called Promise. The promise that Baruch possessed was that God would be with him and would spare his life.

That's what happened. The lives of Jeremiah and Baruch were marvelously spared. Jehoiakim sent a posse after them, but could not find them. The Bible says simply, "The Lord hid them" (36:26, KJV).

F.B. Meyer comments, "The divine hidings are needed by us all. We are too prominent, too self-important, too conscious of ourselves. Our shadows fall too much in front of us. . . . God must sometimes hide us in the sick chamber, the valley of the shadow, the cleft of the rock."

Where God hid Jeremiah and Baruch we don't know. Perhaps it was literally in a cleft of the rock. But we *do* know what they did in hiding. "Take thee another roll and write," God said to Jeremiah, who relayed the message to Baruch. For both of them, it meant getting back to work—good medicine for two discouraged, depressed people.

Chapter 36 ends with the words: "Baruch . . . wrote therein

from the mouth of Jeremiah all the words of the book which Jehoiakim, king of Judah had burned in the fire: and there were added besides unto them many like words" (v. 32, KJV). I like that last part.

You can't get rid of God's Word by throwing it into the fire. It keeps coming back from the ashes. And when it comes back, it comes back with reinforcements.

Like Baruch, you may wonder at times if your work is worth the effort. You may have written that scroll a dozen times and each time it is torn up and thrown in the fire. What's the use? How many times can you face repeated rejection?

But God promises you, as He promised Baruch, that He is not only a Comforting Presence and a Continuing Protector, but He is also the Powerful Overcomer. There may be a dozen losses along the way, but God doesn't count wins and losses like a baseball manager. He has His eye on the ultimate victory.

"Be of good cheer, blessed and happy Baruch, I am not only with you to the end of the world, I am also the Overcomer of that world."

9

The View from the Hiding Place

Jeremiah 13; 46—49; 22:1—23:8

One of my prize possessions is an autographed copy of Corrie
ten Boom's book, *A Prisoner and Yet.* It was published in the
1950s, years before she became famous for the publication of
The Hiding Place.

Both books tell substantially the same story. In her home in
the Nazi-occupied Netherlands, Corrie and her family provided a hiding place for Jewish refugees. The entrance to the
hiding place was through Corrie's closet. "Under the bottom
shelf," she writes in *A Prisoner and Yet,* "was a sliding door,
behind which was the secret space where approximately eight
people could stand."

Regularly, they practiced "safety drills," which Corrie says,
"were tremendously important. With a stopwatch in hand, I
would stand by, while everyone disappeared into my
closet. . . . Seventy seconds it took them. I made the rounds of
the rooms. They looked uninhabited, the mattresses turned
over, the blankets folded underneath. The sheets were taken
along into hiding. . . ."

"It was a pity that we had to have these drills," Corrie
continues. "We all felt keenly the tragic necessity of them, and
so I used to ease the situation by treating the group to cream
puffs" (Christian Literature Crusade, p. 12).

There is something very romantic about cream puffs and secret hiding places, unless you are hiding from the Nazis like Corrie ten Boom—or unless you were hiding from King Jehoiakim like Jeremiah and Baruch.

Where Jeremiah and Baruch hid is unknown; it is also unknown how long they remained in hiding. But we can make some educated guesses. The only travel referred to in the Book of Jeremiah that doesn't have a clear time frame is a trip mentioned in chapter 13. Some commentators feel that Baruch and Jeremiah took this mysterious trip while they were evading Jehoiakim's posse.

Still Hiding Out
The story in Jeremiah 13 is seemingly insignificant. Most of our English versions indicate that Jeremiah traveled to the Euphrates River, at least 350 miles away, to bury a waistcloth, and later returned to dig it up again. Scholars have been debating whether the trip was literal or not, and whether he really went to the Euphrates River. If it was literal, Jeremiah walked two round trips, a total of at least 1,400 miles, all for the purpose of acting out a parable.

Some Bible versions provide a marginal note that the word translated Euphrates is Perath or the Hebrew letters PRH. Perhaps Jeremiah was not referring to the River Euphrates— he doesn't say river—but to another place nearer to his hometown of Anathoth. George Adam Smith says, "Within an hour from Anathoth lies the Wadi Farah, a name which corresponds to the Hebrew Parath or (by a slight change) Parah; and the Wadi, familiar as it must have been to Jeremiah suits the picture, having a lavish fountain, a broad pool and a stream; all of which soak into the sand and fissured rock of the surrounding desert. That the Wadi Farah was the scene of the parable is therefore possible, though not certain."

Smith admits that the details are ambiguous. But, of course, if Perath was the hiding place for Jeremiah and Baruch, it would be well for it to be ambiguous. He and Baruch may have been able to slip in and out of Jerusalem for occasional supplies, but God kept them hidden in Perath.

The point of the story in chapter 13, which Jeremiah explained when he returned briefly to Jerusalem, is simply this: Just as an undergarment is close to a person, so Judah had been close to God. The waistcloth was of linen, a material associated with the priesthood, and Israel was called a "kingdom of priests" (Ex. 19:6). They were to be a "people, a name, a praise, and a glory" (Jer. 13:11, RSV). Instead, the whole nation was going to be taken into exile (to Perath which stood for the Euphrates) where the Lord would "spoil the pride of Judah" as the waistcloth itself had been spoiled (v. 9, RSV).

You may already have noticed that Jeremiah was always down-to-earth. Ezekiel had visions of a wheel in a wheel way up in the middle of the air. Isaiah saw the Lord high and lifted up with His glory filling the temple. But Jeremiah had object lessons about broken jars, baskets of rotten figs, and waistcloths.

God speaks in all aspects of life. He can ordain the commonplace and infuse the secular with His holiness. The kitchen and the factory can bring Him glory as well as the sanctuary and the prayer closet. Ezekiel is no more sacred because he had esoteric visions, nor is the ordinary in our lives to be despised because it is mundane.

As for hiding places, while they usually begin romantically, they become boring rather quickly. Elijah was fed by ravens by the Brook Cherith, and for the first few weeks that must have been exciting; but then the novelty wore off. For the Israelites in the wilderness, even manna lost its charm (Num. 1:5-6).

Though hiding places have their limitations, they can be excellent sites for viewing things in proper perspective. In the turbulence of daily living, you often concern yourself with coping. In a hiding place, you can get a broader view. Life's petty details lose significance. What once seemed so important is now inconsequential.

While he was in his hiding place, Jeremiah probably dictated some of his prophecies regarding the nations (Jer. 46—49).

These prophecies speak of the future of Egypt, Philistia, Moab, Ammon, and a few other nations. During this time he had some clearer insights into the character of King Jehoiakim; these insights are expressed in Jeremiah 22:13—23.

In Jerusalem, Jeremiah had been a participant; in his hiding place, he was an observer. What did he observe?

He saw King Jehoiakim trembling under the immanence of Nebuchadnezzar's attack and becoming a vassal of the Babylonian leader (see 2 Kings 24:1). However, he also saw that as soon as the Babylonian army left the area, Jehoiakim started mending fences with Egypt, his neighbor to the southwest. To Jeremiah this was foolish, perfidious, and extremely hazardous.

But what struck Jeremiah was that the most important ingredient in the makeup of a monarch should be righteousness, but that was certainly not the most significant ingredient in Jehoiakim's makeup. Of course, it is a plus if the ruler is wise and politically astute. Of course, it is important that he is respected and honored. But most important is that he give a priority to righteousness. No matter how you look at it, King Jehoiakim didn't measure up.

Act Justly and Fairly

In chapters 21—24, the prophet repeatedly emphasizes the importance of righteousness. And how do you measure the righteousness of a leader? Jeremiah says that it is in helping the little man, the down-and-outer, the struggler, the person forgotten by society. This is the mark of righteousness; and this is the characteristic of good leadership.

In Jeremiah 21:12, the prophet says, "Rescue from the hand of his oppressor the one who has been robbed." Later he says, "Deal justly and fairly . . . do not ill-treat or do violence to the alien, the orphan, or the widow, do not shed innocent blood in this place" (22:3, NEB).

Our society is built on pressure groups. Political lobbies and power blocs push to get their bills signed into law. But Jeremiah says that the righteous leader is the one who cares for those who have no pressure group to lobby for them.

The politics of power infects the church as well. Too often, decisions are made on the strength of the power bloc pushing for it; those who have no one to care are forgotten.

We live our lives according to what is most convenient and most beneficial for our present and future tranquility rather than for what Jeremiah calls righteousness. But what if the majority doesn't care about the aliens, orphans, and widows? What if the majority feels that the church would be happier and grow faster without such people?

Jeremiah would say, "Live righteously." As he looked at Jehoiakim, he certainly didn't see a paragon of righteousness. Instead, speaking of his ruler, he says, "Woe to him who builds his palace by unrighteousness, his upper rooms by injustice, making his countrymen work for nothing, not paying them for their labor" (v. 13).

Jeremiah is saying that instead of aiding the underprivileged, Jehoiakim was pressing them into slavery, a violation of the Mosaic law (Lev. 19:13; Deut. 24:14-15).

South of Jerusalem, near Bethlehem, at Ramat Rahel, Jehoiakim was building a personal fortress for himself. It was panelled with expensive cedar and painted bright red. Jehoiakim must have thought that future historians would look at that mansion and exclaim, "What a magnificent monarch he must have been!"

But Jeremiah says that it is not the quantity of cedar you have or the brightness of your red paint that makes you a great leader. What counts is whether you rule justly and righteously. Jehoiakim's father, Josiah, was concerned about justice; Jehoiakim was concerned about himself.

I admit that it's not a nice thing to say, but evangelicals today resemble Jehoiakim in more ways than one. We too are often more concerned about our material possessions than we are about eternal things. Indeed, we are more concerned with our houses and lands than we are with the crucial issues of this world. Just as Jehoiakim ignored Nebuchadnezzar while working on his grand palace, so we today are often absorbed with selfish and personal concerns and care little about the concerns—nuclear, environmental, totalitarian—that threaten our society.

Like Jehoiakim, we also have a tendency to think of ourselves rather than to think of the poor and underprivileged. A century ago the church had a similar preoccupation with itself. It had gotten to accept the notion of foreign missions; indeed there was a glamor attached to the "foreign field." After all, the poor and underprivileged were easier to acknowledge when they were thousands of miles away than when they were on your doorstep.

In such an atmosphere, William and Catherine Booth launched their East London Mission, which later evolved into the Salvation Army. The church gave them very little support; the government didn't want to acknowledge that there was a problem. But the Booths knew there was a problem that wouldn't go away. William Booth was pelted with garbage by the drunkards of the East End, and he took his son into a pub, saying, "These are our people. These are the people I want to live for and bring to Christ."

Times haven't changed much. It is still too easy to push the poor into ghettoes and forget about them. We don't think of "neglect of the poor" as being a sin, and if it is, we certainly don't consider it a major one. We like to draw up our own lists of sin. The sins that the other fellow is prone to commit are heinous; the sins that beset us are trivial.

God's Word embarrassingly groups all sins together. On one of his lists, the Apostle Paul combines gossip with murder (Rom. 1:29-30, MLB). Jeremiah puts neglect of the poor as a sin of the highest magnitude. On our lists it would probably be only a footnote.

The Meaning of Righteousness
Jeremiah and Baruch may have remained in hiding for the rest of Jehoiakim's reign, observing the continual decline of any semblance of national righteousness. At the age of 36, King Jehoiakim died—unloved, unwanted, and not even honored

by a decent burial. It was as Jeremiah had prophesied he would die. His son Jehoiachin took the throne in 597 B.C., but he paid the price for his father's double cross of Nebuchadnezzar. After reigning only three months, Jehoiachin was deposed by the Babylonian monarch and carted off to Babylon.

It was no great loss. However, Nebuchadnezzar did far more than take Jehoiachin into captivity. He also ransacked both the city of Jerusalem and its renowned temple. The sad scene is depicted by the writer of the Book of Kings: "And he carried out from there all the treasures of the house of the Lord, and the treasures of the king's house, and cut in pieces all the vessels of gold which Solomon King of Israel had made in the temple of the Lord, just as the Lord had said. Then he led away into exile all Jerusalem and all the captains and all the mighty men of valor, 10,000 captives, and all the craftsmen and the smiths. None remained except the poorest people of the land" (2 Kings 24:13-14, NASB). Along with the poorest people of the land were Jeremiah and Baruch.

Jeremiah had witnessed the fulfillment of many of his prophecies, but that didn't make him any happier. He loved Jerusalem and its temple. In many ways, he would have liked to have gone into captivity with the others. But instead he remained in the city with the poor and the outcasts.

Why wasn't Jeremiah taken into captivity? Perhaps because his prophecies had become known to Nebuchadnezzar, or perhaps because he had been in a hiding place and had not been a resident of Jerusalem during most of the previous five years. Otherwise, Baruch from a noble family and Jeremiah from a priestly family would have been taken into exile.

Nebuchadnezzar installed on the throne a member of the royal family named Mattaniah. Nebuchadnezzar knew that he would not be a threat to raise a serious insurrection. Mattaniah was a weakling and he was surrounded by a cabinet of incompetents. The most auspicious thing that Mattaniah did was to change his name to Zedekiah, which means, "Jehovah my Righteousness." If ever Judah needed righteousness in its leadership, it was now.

Now was a good time for Jeremiah to come out of hiding. Some commentators feel that Jeremiah 22—23 are sort of an inauguration sermon for the new king. Certainly, some of the material had been presented before to previous monarchs. But now it may have been assembled and collated and presented in one piece to Zedekiah.

Once again Jeremiah stressed that justice and righteousness are priorities of government, and these are evidenced in how leaders treat the downtrodden and underprivileged. Now there were more downtrodden and underprivileged in Jerusalem than ever before.

When the prophet finished reviewing the perfidious unrighteousness of Zedekiah's predecessors (Shallum, Jehoiakim, and Jehoiachin—three ignominious rulers in a 12-year span) and as he looked ahead to the weak man on the throne who called himself "Jehovah my Righteousness," he despaired about any possibilities from this royal line of David.

But God gave Jeremiah a ray of hope. The Messiah would come, a king who would "reign and prosper" and would "execute judgment and justice in the earth" (23:5, KJV). He is called the "Righteous Branch," and He would truly bear the name "The Lord our Righteousness" *(Jehovah Tsidkenu).*

Jeremiah knew that human righteousness does not exist in any absolute sense. "The heart is deceitful above all things and desperately wicked; who can know it?" (17:9, KJV) he had said years earlier. Isaiah had previously declared, "All our righteousnesses are as filthy rags" (Isa. 64:6, KJV), and Jeremiah would probably have said they were like soiled waistcloths. The common people, the priests, the prophets, the kings, and even Jeremiah himself fell far short of God's demands for perfection. Who could possibly reach God's standards? How could man partake of God's righteousness?

You usually don't think of Jeremiah as being a Messianic prophet. Isaiah is full of prophecies about the Messiah, and even the Book of Micah mentions Bethlehem as the Messiah's birthplace (Micah 5:2). But what can Jeremiah tell us? He seems so concerned about the sins of his people, that he scarcely has time to bask in the glories of the promised Messiah. But it is precisely because he is so concerned about sin that he has to find a source of righteousness.

Where was it to be found? Certainly not on earth. Only God Himself could provide righteousness, and what a profound Messianic prophecy that is!

I'm sure that Jeremiah didn't understand all the theological ramifications of what he prophesied. It may have been draped in mystery, but when he spoke of the Messiah as the Righteous Branch and called Him the Lord our Righteousness and when he uses the same phrase to refer to His people (Jer. 33:16), you realize that he had an amazing grasp of what we call New Testament truth. He understood at least part of all the aspects of biblical righteousness.

British Bible teacher A.T. Pierson once said, "The primary meaning of righteousness is . . . rightness—rightness of dealing, of judging, of adjustment; rightness of relationship, rightness of conduct and character. And then it comes to mean the investiture of righteousness, as with an attribute; and so it comes to mean acceptableness as righteous before a righteous God. Righteousness includes not only imputation, but impartation. Let us never forget that, when God justifies a sinner, He not only accepts him as right, but He makes Him right."

Basically, then, biblical righteousness has five parts: (1) rightness in dealing; (2) rightness in relationship; (3) rightness in conduct and character; then as we confess our inabililty to measure up to God's standards and as we see our inability to establish a relationship with Him by our own conduct and character, we ask to be clothed in the righteousness provided by Him in Jesus Christ. Then (4) He invests us with His divine righteousness and we are accepted before Him; and finally (5) He imparts righteousness to us, and the Holy Spirit takes residence within us and we partake of the divine nature. We become a new creation (2 Cor. 5:17); Christ lives in us (Gal. 2:20); and thus we become "servants of righteousness" (Rom. 6:18, KJV). It's all wrapped up in the profound verse: "He made Him who knew no sin to be sin on our behalf, that we might become the righteousness of God in Him" (2 Cor. 5:21, NASB).

Donald Grey Barnhouse used the illustration that if you look through a piece of red glass, everything is red; through blue glass, everything is blue; through yellow glass, everything is yellow. When God looks at us, He sees us in Jesus Christ. We take on the characteristics of Jesus Christ. We are clothed in His righteousness. His righteousness becomes ours. Paul writes: "Christ . . . is made unto us . . . righteousness" (1 Cor. 1:30, KJV).

It was a truth that was difficult for John Bunyan, author of *Pilgrim's Progress,* to grasp. Even after his conversion, he was plagued with doubts and lived a life of fear and defeat. In his autobiography *Grace Abounding,* he tells about it: "One day, as I was passing in the field, and that too with some dashes on my conscience, fearing lest yet all was not right, suddenly this sentence fell upon my soul, 'Thy righteousness is in heaven,' and . . . I saw with the eyes of my soul, Jesus Christ at God's right hand; there, I say, is my righteousness. . . . I also saw, moreover, that it was not my good frame of heart that made my righteousness better, nor yet my bad frame that made my righteousness worse; for my righteousness was Jesus Christ Himself, the same yesterday and today and forever. . . . Now I went home rejoicing, 'Thy righteousness is in heaven, thy righteousness is in heaven.' "

Another who discovered this truth was Robert Murray McCheyne. He was only 18 and a student at Edinburg University. His brother, David, 26, had just passed away and Robert was heartbroken. His brother David had prayed often for him. Even one sin, his brother had told him, could keep him out of heaven, and Robert knew that he had many more sins than that to account for.

Robert couldn't sleep; he couldn't concentrate on his studies; he could think only of his own sinfulness. He knew what he had to do. It was what his brother had often urged him to do: put his trust in Jesus Christ and ask Him to become His righteousness. He did.

Shortly afterward, he wrote the following lines:
I once was a stranger to grace and to God;
I knew not my danger, and felt not my load;
Though friends spoke in rapture of Christ on the
    tree,
"Jehovah Tsidkenu" was nothing to me.

Like tears from the daughters of Zion that roll,
I wept when the waters went over His soul,
Yet thought not that my sins had nailed to the tree
"Jehovah Tsidkenu"—'twas nothing to me.

When free grace awoke me, by light from on high,
Then legal fears shook me, I trembled to die:
No refuge, no safety, in self could I see;
"Jehovah Tsidkenu" my Saviour must be.

My terrors all vanished before the sweet name;
My guilty fears banished, with boldness I came
To drink at the fountain, life-giving and free:
"Jehovah Tsidkenu" was all things to me.

"Jehovah Tsidkenu!" My treasure and boast;
"Jehovah Tsidkenu!" I ne'er can be lost;
In Thee I shall conquer by flood and by field—
My Cable, my Anchor, my Breastplate and Shield!

E'en treading the valley, the shadow of death,
This watchword shall rally my faltering breath;
For, when from life's fever my God sets me free,
"Jehovah Tsidkenu" my death-song shall be.

10

I Never Liked
True-False Tests

Jeremiah 14; 27—29; 23:9-40

No, I never did.

Everyone else thought that they were easy. They told me that you had a 50-50 chance on every question, and that those were the best odds that you could expect from a teacher. But for some reason, it never worked out for me.

If the question was: "True or False: Christopher Columbus discovered America in 1492," I would imagine that it was probably a trick question. Maybe his name really wasn't Christopher Columbus. Was it really America that he discovered in 1492 or was it merely a few islands in the Caribbean? And are we sure it all happened in 1492?

By the time I had pondered all the angles long enough, I invariably answered the question exactly the opposite from the way the teacher had intended. The harder I tried to avoid error, the more surely I plunged myself into it.

I had another system that proved just as disastrous. Whenever I came across a difficult true-false question, I would look to see what answers I had given the previous three questions. If the three previous questions had all been marked true, than I figured that by the law of averages this one should be marked false. But I discovered through my high school years that teachers were inveterate violators of the law of averages.

How do you avoid error anyway? Even more important than school exams, how do you avoid serious error in life?

Of course, you can find people who say that it doesn't matter which answers you choose. Everything is relative, they say. There are no wrong answers. Some answers may be slightly preferable to others, but none are wrong. Go any way you wish and run down the path no matter where it leads.

Well, I sometimes tried to persuade teachers that the answer could be either true or false, but most teachers wouldn't fall for the line. Most of them said something like this: "Either Columbus discovered America in 1492 or he didn't. You can't have it both ways."

That's what Jeremiah was saying in 594 B.C. You can't have it both ways.

It's easy from our vantage point to acknowledge that Jeremiah had the right answers and his opponents were all wrong. But if you had lived in Jeremiah's time, you might have been as befuddled as I was with the true and false tests.

The Summit Conference

Put yourself in the sandals of the people in Jerusalem in 594 B.C. It was a summit conference for nonaligned nations. The nations weren't really nonaligned, but they wanted to be. By force, Nebuchadnezzar had signed them up to be his allies 5 or 10 years earlier. Allies isn't the right word either; maybe vassals would be better.

Now they were growing restless. Nebuchadnezzar was 800 miles away. To bring the strength of his army to put down an insurrection in Palestine would take months. Perhaps if they pooled their forces, perhaps if they recruited Egypt to be on their side, they might be able to throw off the yoke of Nebuchadnezzar.

The time was ripe. Nebuchadnezzar was having some internal problems that year; a bit of a civil war was giving him headaches, and he was just finishing up a military campaign to the east. So a rebellion in the west made sense.

Through the years these nonaligned powers had fought

each other, but now they had a common enemy. If they worked with each other for a change, they might be able to get their freedom back.

What Nebuchadnezzar did to Judah—take the cream of the native talent into exile, loot the treasures of the capital, and install a puppet in power—he had done to the other minor kingdoms as well. But the puppets didn't want their strings pulled any longer.

So they converged on Jerusalem. From the south came envoys and ambassadors from Edom, Moab, and Ammon; from the north came envoys and ambassadors from Tyre and Sidon. They met in Jerusalem—not because King Zedekiah was a strong leader, nor because he was the agitator of the planned rebellion—but because Jerusalem was central.

However, an uninvited guest came to their party. As welcome as ants at a picnic, there was Jeremiah, the veteran prophet. Jeremiah was in his mid-50s now and had been on his soapbox for more than 30 years. Zedekiah was the fifth monarch to whom he had brought the Word of the Lord. Unlike Jehoiakim who had sent Jeremiah and Baruch scurrying into hiding, King Zedekiah seemed somewhat receptive to Jeremiah's message. At times he even consulted with Jeremiah. Of course, he seldom did what Jeremiah counseled, but that may have been because he always consulted with his cabinet after he consulted with Jeremiah, and the two never agreed.

Thus the summit conference for nonaligned powers was convened against the advice of Jeremiah and with Zedekiah unsure of what he really wanted to do. With Jeremiah, however, there was absolutely no uncertainty. He knew he wouldn't be invited to the summit to make a speech, so he had to get his message across some other way—some graphic way, some way that would grab everyone's attention.

A Wooden Yoke

Directed by the Lord, Jeremiah made a yoke—wooden bars held together by leather thongs, similar to the kind that oxen wore in the field. Placing it around his neck and across his shoulders, he preached his message as the delegates passed by. The message was clear. The nations were intending to throw off Nebuchadnezzar's yoke: Jeremiah was saying that they should continue to wear it.

A revolt would be both wrong and futile, Jeremiah said. It would be wrong because each of the countries had pledged to Nebuchadnezzar that they would submit to him; now they were planning a rebellion. It would be futile because God had appointed Nebuchadnezzar to be His instrument of judgment. To get his point across to the representatives of the foreign powers, Jeremiah emphasized that his message came not from a local tribal deity, but rather from the omnipotent God of the universe who with His "great power and outstretched arm" made the earth, its people, and all the animal kingdom.

Jeremiah knew what the local prophets, diviners, dream merchants, and fortune-tellers were saying. They were encouraging the summit conference. But Jeremiah said that his message came directly from the Almighty God. Failure to submit to God's will would bring "sword, famine, and plague" (Jer. 14:12). Whether they liked it or not, Nebuchadnezzar was God's instrument.

But they didn't like it and they didn't heed God's warnings.

After the summit conference, Jeremiah repeated the same message to his own monarch, Zedekiah: "Keep the yoke of Nebuchadnezzar on you. Don't listen to the false prophets. If you do, you will perish." When Jeremiah finished warning Zedekiah, he went to the priests and the people: "Don't be fooled by the false prophets. The hope they hold out is not from God."

As an inhabitant of Jerusalem, you might understandably be confused. Granted, Jeremiah was right when he had prophesied that Nebuchadnezzar would conquer Jerusalem, but did that necessarily mean that he was right now? After all, he was in the minority, and a minority of one at that. All the soothsayers and astrologers of the neighboring nations were saying that now was the time to revolt. Of course, you don't usually listen to those pagan diviners, but when they all say the same thing, it has to make you think, doesn't it? Don't you think they might know something that Jeremiah didn't know?

Besides that, it was logical. Nebuchadnezzar's hold on his own country seemed to be breaking up. News reports told of increasing internal unrest in Babylon. He was also being attacked from the outside. According to rumors, Syria in the north was planning some kind of insurrection. If ever there was a logical time to revolt, this was it. And there was a theological reason too. Certainly God would want His people free, wouldn't He?

Sincerely Wrong

During the next several weeks, Jeremiah kept wearing his homemade yoke. What a spectacle he was making of himself! But he certainly didn't have to say much. The people knew exactly what his message was.

Then one day in late summer, a prophet named Hananiah came to town. Unhappy with Jeremiah's unpatriotic message, he addressed the crowds in the temple with a strong message to counteract what Jeremiah had been prophesying: "This is what the Lord told me: 'I will break the yoke of the king of Babylon. Within two years all the exiles will return, King Jehoiachin will be back and all the articles that Nebuchadnezzar has taken will be returned to their places in the temple.' "

In the crowd was Jeremiah, still wearing his heavy yoke. The people were responding warmly, even enthusiastically, to Hananiah's message. Jeremiah wasn't surprised. In fact, when the last Amen was said, Jeremiah himself shouted, "Amen."

Suddenly the crowd hushed. Had Jeremiah changed his prophecy? Had he finally seen the light?

But Jeremiah had more to say. "Amen," he continued. "I wish that what Hananiah prophesied would really take place. But it won't. Prophets long before us have predicted war, disaster, and plague for this nation if it pursued a course of idolatry and adultery. I was not the first of the prophets. Hananiah, you are the one out of step, not me."

Suddenly, Hananiah had lost his audience, and so he responded quickly to gain it back. Dramatically, he marched to Jeremiah, took the yoke from the prophet's neck, and vigorously broke it. "That's the way the Lord will break the yoke of Nebuchadnezzar. And it will happen within two years."

Jeremiah stood mute. In the hushed silence of the crowd, he slowly walked away. From the crowd's point of view, it must have looked as if Hananiah had won the argument.

But a short time later, the two men met again. This time the Lord gave Jeremiah words to say and he used them effectively: "Hananiah, you may have broken a wooden yoke, but in its place God will put an iron yoke on this people. And you, Hananiah, will die before the year is out."

Which prophet would you have believed? Hananiah's credentials were similar to Jeremiah's. He came from a town not far from Anathoth, where Jeremiah had grown up. He probably had a similar lineage in a priestly line, even as Jeremiah had. Hananiah spoke in Jehovah's name, and he used the same kind of words that Jeremiah used. His logic seemed sound; he had a good reputation; everyone seemed to like him; he was certainly much more popular than Jeremiah. He seemed sincere and sure of himself too. The way he broke Jeremiah's yoke proved that he was a prophet who wasn't fooling. If he was faking, do you think he would have been so determined?

Two months later, Hananiah died. It was sudden, shocking, and unexpected by almost everyone.

How to Avoid Error
But there's still more to the story. Not only were there false prophets in Judah and the surrounding nations, but there were also false prophets among the exiled Jews in Babylon.

Shortly after Jeremiah's confrontation with Hananiah, King Zedekiah decided to send a delegation to Babylon (possibly to tell Nebuchadnezzar that he didn't mean any harm by the recent summit conference in Jerusalem) and Jeremiah asked the king's envoys to deliver some mail for him. Today we would call it a diplomatic mail pouch.

In his letter, Jeremiah was trying to counter what the false prophets in Babylon were telling the exiles there. Like Hananiah, they were saying that the Captivity would be finished in a couple of years. Jeremiah's letter emphasized that the Captivity would last 70 years, so they had better settle down, build houses, and plant gardens. Moreover, they should learn to be good citizens in the new land.

A prophet in Babylon named Shemaiah took strong exception to Jeremiah's letter and quickly responded by writing to the new temple overseer in Jerusalem (he was the chief of police, you'll remember). Shemaiah admonished the overseer to have Jeremiah locked up. Obviously, the new overseer was not doing his job, said Shemaiah.

Maybe Jeremiah had been right earlier, but to tell the exiles they should make themselves at home in Babylon and cooperate with the tyrant Nebuchadnezzar demonstrated clearly that Jeremiah had lost his mind. A man like that shouldn't be permitted to roam the streets, and certainly he shouldn't be permitted to use the diplomatic mail pouch to send treasonous messages to the exiles.

Fortunately for Jeremiah, he got wind of what Shemaiah had written. So immediately he shot back two letters to Babylon, one addressed to Mr. Shemaiah, the other addressed to the exiles as a whole. In both letters, Shemaiah was denounced as a false prophet. But if you had lived in Babylonian exile, who would you have believed and who would you have thought the false prophet to be?

It isn't always easy to tell truth from error. When you ask, "Will the real prophet please stand up?" and both of them rise, what do you do? While some false prophets are "con" men, others may be sincere, though misguided. In Jeremiah 14:13-16, utterances of the false prophets are labeled either as lying visions, valueless divinations, or self-deception. In other words, some of them deceived themselves; they had talked themselves into what they thought was God's will. They were deluded by their own wishful thinking.

In chapter 23, Jeremiah speaks of their visions as being self-induced (v. 16). The false prophets were like men, groping in darkness, sliding on a slippery trail, stumbling and falling on each other. They were not in touch with heaven, so they were unable to convey God's decisions to men. In addition, they pandered to evil; rather than denouncing adultery and immorality, they condoned it, excused it, and some of them even espoused it.

In any age God's people need scribes, priests, and prophets who are faithful to the Lord. We need scribes to teach God's Word and instruct us in the understanding of our sacred heritage. We need priests to lead us in worship, to uplift the holy, majestic God, and to show us the sufficient sacrifice that God has provided for us. We also need prophets to strip away the veneer of our religious routines and bring us back to basics.

But the false prophets of Jeremiah's time simply continued traditions; they never challenged them in the light of God's Word. They sanctified the status quo. They mistook their hopes for revelations. They conjectured what they thought *ought* to be and then ordained their notions as God's will.

We always prefer to have our prophets speak against the *other* guy—the Babylonians, the Egyptians, the Communists, the Nazis, the militants; prophets quickly lose their popularity when they speak about the sins of God's people. For this reason, it is difficult for a prophet to succeed on television. Prophets seldom "succeed" anywhere, least of all on TV.

Materialism, for example, is a sin that is too close for comfort. The necessities of life grow every year so that we don't have to feel guilty about our own materialism. Modern-day prophets learn to avoid such matters. The more they confirm our own prejudices, the more we're convinced that they must be the mouthpieces of God. We like it when sin "out there" is denounced, but we shun those who challenge the mores and ingrown peccadillos of our own culture—even our own evangelical culture. We like it when secular humanism is deplored; but we squirm at the notion that we are living comfortably with a secularized Christianity.

However, we still haven't answered the question: How do you avoid error? How do you keep from being led astray by the false prophets? And how do you know a false prophet when you see one?

In Jeremiah 23:25-30, Jehovah is speaking: "I have heard what the prophets say who prophesy lies in My name. They say, 'I had a dream! I had a dream!' How long will this continue in the hearts of these lying prophets, who prophesy the delusions of their own minds? . . . Let the prophet who has a dream tell his dream, but let the one who has My Word speak it faithfully. For what has straw to do with grain? . . . I am against the prophets who steal from one another words supposedly from Me."

That's the difference, says Alexander Stewart in his devotional commentary on Jeremiah. "It is the difference between wheat and chaff. . . . On a hasty view, chaff . . . has the appearance of pure grain . . . but there is a vital difference, the difference between the empty husk and the real staff of life."

God's truth is satisfying; it meets the spiritual hunger of man. The Lord goes on to add, "Is not My Word like fire . . . and like a hammer that breaks a rock in pieces?" (v. 29) The hammer of God's truth may crush us for a time, but His fire melts us, refines us, and then gives divine light. When God says that His truth is like wheat, a hammer, and a fire, you realize that He has provided you with the necessities of life. That's a very valuable package to possess.

Another prophet who lived about the same time as Jeremiah was Habakkuk. Like Jeremiah, he too didn't understand what God was doing. He received the same message that Jeremiah had received: the Babylonians are coming. And it didn't make sense to him. It didn't seem as if this was the way that God should do things. But unlike Hananiah who didn't take time to listen to God, Habakkuk did.

What Habakkuk learned are good guidelines for us as well. First, you should be willing to wait (Hab. 2:1). Most decisions do not need to be made on a whim or on an impulse. Take time to pray and study God's Word.

Second, watch to see what God has already done and what He is doing now (Hab. 2:2-3). This enables you to have a clearer perspective. As you view things, try to look at them from God's point of view, not your own.

Third, you must have faith in Him (Hab. 2:4). "The just shall live by his faith" (KJV) is the verse that God gave Habakkuk. You may not see the fulfillment of God's plan. You may never understand God's purposes for your life, but God still wants you to live your life in humble faith, believing in Him.

Those were the clues that God have Habakkuk. Now let's be a bit more specific for ourselves.

1. Humble yourself. A.W. Tozer once said, "There is a close relation between humility and the perception of truth." The psalmist acknowledged, "The meek will He guide in judgment and the meek will He teach His way" (Ps. 25:9, KJV). In humility, open yourself then to the will of God, even if God's will for you is Nebuchadnezzar.

2. Trust God. When the Apostle Paul lists the Christian's armor in Ephesians 6, he cites faith as our shield. As you put your confidence in the Lord, you can be sure that He will protect you and keep you from error.

3. Check the Word. God never contradicts Himself. He will not lead you one way if His Word indicates another. His will parallels His Word.

Of course, that does not mean that you can take a verse out of context to support your cause. But if you understand and obey His Word, you will be kept from serious error.

4. Pray. "If any of you lack wisdom, let him ask of God that giveth to all men liberally, and upbraideth not; and it shall be given him" (James 1:5, KJV). Make sure, when you pray, to allow God to use you and speak to you; don't try to use God to accomplish your will.

5. Think. God has given you a brain to use, so use it. Dreams and visions are not necessarily more spiritual than sermon sense. God does not want us to put our brains in neutral when we serve Him.

6. Expect the Holy Spirit to give you light. Though the Lord expects you to use your head, He has also given the Holy Spirit to you to lead you into all truth (John 16:13). There is a wisdom that is from above, and divine wisdom transcends human wisdom.

Yes, there is truth, absolute truth, and there is falsehood that needs to be shunned. There are men of God who need to be heeded, and false prophets who need to be avoided. But the Jeremiahs do not usually win popularity contests.

11

Is Anything Too Hard for the Lord?

Jeremiah 21; 37; 30—33

Anything too hard for God?

Of course not, you say. God is omnipotent, omniscient, and omnipresent. He can do anything. He works miracles.

The question is still a good one for two reasons: first, it's a question that is asked a couple of times in Scripture, and second, it's a question that God asks of us when we are going through deep waters and when our faith is strained to the breaking point.

In Scripture, this question was first asked way back in the Book of Genesis. God had just told 100-year-old Abraham that his 90-year-old wife Sarah would bear a son before another year had passed. Sarah had overheard the conversation and the Bible says she "laughed to herself" (Gen. 18:12).

You have to admit it did seem funny; in fact, it was downright impossible for a 90-year-old woman to become pregnant and bear a child. If a gynecologist had predicted it, he would have been drummed out of the A.M.A. But it was God who said it.

Sarah thought she was laughing to herself, but it is difficult to keep anything to yourself when God is around, which is all the time. So God responded with a question, "Is anything too hard for the Lord?" (v. 14) Within the year, a baby boy was

117

born to two very senior citizens.

"I Need a Miracle!"

Now the year is 589 B.C. Jeremiah is about 57 years old. For 35 years he has been a prophet and he hasn't seen a miracle yet. Oh, he's seen trash heaps, broken pots, waistcloths, and rotten fruit—but no miracles.

The current monarch, Zedekiah, has been on the throne for 8 years. At 29, he is still an inept ruler, led by a foolish band of officials who compose his cabinet. Easily swayed by public opinion, he is aware that many of his citizens regard the exiled Jehoiachin as the legitimate monarch. So Zedekiah tries harder to win the public's affection.

Five years earlier he had plans to rebel, but when Nebuchadnezzar caught wind of those plans, Zedekiah quickly shelved the idea. Immediately, envoys were dispatched to assure Nebuchadnezzar of his loyalty; then he traveled to Babylon himself (Jer. 51:59) for the same purpose.

Now four years after that abortive revolt, King Zedekiah has gotten braver again. Maybe foolhardy is a more appropriate term. A new Pharaoh (Hophra) has come to the throne in Egypt and is egging Zedekiah and his cabinet to action. The neighboring states of Tyre and Ammon are also eager to throw off the Babylonian yoke.

It doesn't take long, however, before Nebuchadnezzar's troops start moving westward into Palestine. One by one, the fortified cities throughout Judah and Philistia fall to the overwhelming forces of the occupying army. The gruesome details of the invasion are adequately documented by archeological research.

Now it is January 588 B.C. The Babylonian army has ringed Jerusalem, blockading it so that food supplies cannot be brought in from the surrounding countryside. Always unsure of himself, Zedekiah had second thoughts about everything; now he has second thoughts about his plans for rebellion. Where can he turn for help?

He has sought military help from Egypt, but none has come;

most of the smaller states in the area have either already been devastated or else are quaking in their boots. What Zedekiah needs is a miracle. So he sends messengers to Jeremiah, asking for a miracle (21:2). He knows that the members of his cabinet won't appreciate his contact with the prophet, but when you're desperate you seek help wherever you can.

That's how the situation stood for the king; now consider how it was for the prophet. Commentator George Adam Smith looks at Jeremiah's predicament: "History has no harder test for the character and doctrine of a great teacher than the siege of his city. . . . A siege brings the prophet's feet as low as the feet of the crowd. He shares the dangers, the duties of defense, the last crusts. His hunger, and what is still keener, his pity for those who suffer it with him, may break his faith into cowardice and superstition."

Of course, Jeremiah can still defect to the Babylonian forces if he wants to; he would be treated as a hero by Babylon. But that's the last thing he wants. Instead, he prefers to share "the last crusts" in Jerusalem. These are his people; this is his city. He may predict its destruction; he may advise his people to surrender, but he is staying to the end. Just as Elijah suffered from the shortages of the three-year drought he had predicted, so Jeremiah suffers the hunger pangs of the Babylonian blockade.

Now he is requested to intercede for Zedekiah. The king knew his history; so does the prophet. In the ninth century B.C. a king asked for help from the Prophet Elisha and he got it; the nation was spared as a result. About 150 years later, King Hezekiah went to Isaiah for help and got it; once again the nation was spared. Now another 115 years have passed, and Zedekiah, weak and vacillating though he may be, turns to the Prophet Jeremiah and asks for help.

God has delivered the nation in the past. Can He do it again? Is anything too hard for the Lord? Should Jeremiah intercede to God for his people?

Oh, he has been interceding for 35 years; he knows God's answers. He has heard them over and over again. Jeremiah has no miracle-bag from which to pull a miracle, and Jeremiah also knows that there is one thing God cannot do: He cannot go back on His Word. His faithfulness cuts both ways.

So Jeremiah responds, "God Himself will join forces with the Babylonians and will fight against Jerusalem with an outstretched hand and a strong arm." What Zedekiah should do is surrender to the enemy. The section closes, "God will show . . . no mercy, nor pity, nor compassion."

Jeremiah must have been in mental agony as he uttered those words. These were *his* people; this was *his* country; this was *his* beloved city, and in it was the glorious temple of Solomon where Jehovah God was worshiped. To think of all this in ruins must have devastated Jeremiah's sensitive soul.

Gradually, Nebuchadnezzar's noose tightened around the city; the blockade became more impenetrable. The city verged on mass starvation. By now, all the outlying towns and cities except two had been taken, and for those two it was just a matter of time.

Now Jeremiah receives another word from the Lord; it is directed to King Zedekiah, and it is not good news. Jerusalem will be taken and burned; Zedekiah himself will be captured and taken into exile. There is no hope of escape.

The dark winter passes. Now it is spring, and Nebuchadnezzar's forces still have not seized Jerusalem. Then a little sunshine. Egypt's Pharaoh Hophra belatedly orders his army to march into Palestine; it's enough to divert Nebuchadnezzar's attention, and the stranglehold on Jerusalem is eased.

Some Jews believe that a miracle is taking place, but Jeremiah knows better. Nebuchadnezzar will soon be back to finish the job, he tells another delegation sent by King Zedekiah. "Don't fool yourself. Even if Nebuchadnezzar had only wounded soldiers fighting for him, he would win." The miracle that King Zedekiah is hoping for will not take place.

Arrested and Jailed

Taking advantage of the respite, Jeremiah walks out the city gate. In his hometown of Anathoth, a family gathering is convening. A relative has died during the recent turmoil and all family members are asked to come and check out the estate of the deceased which was to be divided among them.

But Jeremiah doesn't get there. At the city gate he is arrested and charged with desertion. For such a long time he has been urging his people to surrender to the enemy that the soldiers are convinced that Jeremiah is intending to do it himself. And nothing he can say will convince them otherwise. He is beaten, probably the most severe beating he has received in his life. Then he is imprisoned in a dungeon underneath the house of the country's secretary of state.

Days pass; then weeks. The damp dungeon is infested with insects and rodents. Jeremiah has no bed; at night he lies down on the cold, slimy floor. Food is dropped to him from above; his health is weakening gradually. His bones ache; he finds it hard to stand up. All the time he is praying to God for deliverance. But there are no miracles for Jeremiah. So he waits and talks with God about it.

Above ground, the Babylonians have now returned in force; once again they have set up a blockade around the city. Though the residents had been able to bring in some food supplies during the respite, they know the prospects are not good. Ahead of them is either starvation or surrender.

King Zedekiah knows it too. His cabinet members tell him that the Egyptians might return and scare the Babylonians away. Zedekiah's confidence in his cabinet's advice is now close to zero. He wants to talk to Jeremiah, but he is afraid. Someone—a member of his cabinet perhaps—might see him. So he arranges a secret meeting. He knows where Jeremiah is. He asks one of his trusted servants to bring Jeremiah secretly to the palace.

The aging prophet, now emaciated and stooped by his latest ordeal, appears before the young monarch. After the official greetings, the king asks a single question: "Is there any word from the Lord?" But there isn't. God's plans haven't changed. "King Zedekiah," the prophet says, "you will soon be handed over to the king of Babylon."

If only Jeremiah could deliver a different message, a message of deliverance instead of doom, he wouldn't have to go back to the dungeon. Instead, the king would release him and honor him; he might even be given a position in the king's cabinet. But for Jeremiah, compromise is not possible. He has no choice but to convey God's message.

However, before Jeremiah leaves the king, he asks Zedekiah what he now thinks of his false prophets—false prophets who had been promising the moon. There's no answer. Then Jeremiah suggests that the least a good king can do would be to provide a better prison for a true prophet.

Surprisingly, King Zedekiah obliges; instead of returning Jeremiah to the dungeon, he is sent to the court of the guard, located next to the king's palace. It is still a prison, but there is fresh air, and the king guarantees him bread to eat for as long as the nation's supplies last.

Jeremiah's new prison has a different set of problems. No privacy. He feels he is in a corral where animals are kept. Soldiers mill around and, not having much else to laugh at, mock the prophet, who now looks two decades older than his years.

A Worthless Purchase?

At this point, the story line jumps to Jeremiah 32—33. A visitor comes. It's a cousin named Hanamel. He brings Jeremiah up-to-date on the developments at the family gathering that Jeremiah didn't attend. After talk of the family, Hanamel makes Jeremiah an offer.

Hanamel needs money. Everything is scarce in Jerusalem; food prices have soared. To stay alive, cousin Hanamel needs some shekels. All he owns is some rather worthless property in Anathoth, probably gotten at the recent family gathering.

It doesn't make any sense for Jeremiah to buy it. Why should he help out a family member? His family had turned against him years earlier. He certainly doesn't owe them any favors. Besides that, Babylonian troops have already overrun the land. So the property is worthless.

But Jeremiah has received word from the Lord to buy the field, and so once again he obeys in spite of the circumstances. And despite the fact that Jerusalem is in a state of economic collapse and its complete destruction is not far in the future, the real estate transaction is handled in a very businesslike manner.

Seven ounces of silver are weighed out; a deed is written; a copy is made; Jeremiah signs his name and puts his seal on in the presence of witnesses. Only one of the copies is sealed, the other is left open. Both are given to Baruch for safekeeping in the presence of witnesses. Both documents are to be preserved in an earthenware jar similar to the way the Dead Sea Scrolls were later preserved by the Qumran community.

You can imagine the scoffing and laughing after the deal was consummated. The soldiers may have been watching silently during the purchase ceremony, but now that it was over, they must have burst out in loud guffaws. "The old prophet has gone off his rocker," they must have thought if not said.

The Hebrews always enjoyed making deals and transactions and they treated them as a spectator sport, cheering the victor when it was over. There is no question who won this one. Hanamel had taken advantage of a mentally deranged old man.

But Jeremiah was not mentally deranged. He knew perfectly well what he was doing, though he may not have understood why. After the transaction is completed and the laughter of the soldier guards has subsided, Jeremiah has a heart-to-heart talk with the Lord about it. Both Jeremiah's prayer and the Lord's response are fascinating.

The prayer begins very properly with a lengthy ascription of praise to God. Jeremiah talks of God's power: "Nothing is too hard for You." He talks of God's grace: "You show love to thousands." He talks of God's wisdom: "Your eyes are open to all the ways of men." He talks of God's mighty acts in history: "You brought Your people Israel out of Egypt with signs and wonders." And he acknowledges the sins of God's people in spite of God's goodness: "They did not do what You commanded them to do" (32:17-25).

Then as he considers the sinfulness of his people, he is reminded of the Babylonian armies and the siege ramps they are building. "They are coming against the city to take it. Surely You see it, Lord. And yet You have told me to buy this worthless land. I don't understand it, Lord."

Interesting, isn't it, that though Jeremiah is obedient, he still has questions. Living a life of faith doesn't mean that you won't have problems or difficulties. Even prophets have their moments of discouragement.

But you may wonder about Jeremiah. Shouldn't he have known God's plan by now? Hadn't God revealed it to him? Well, it's one thing to talk of God's plan and purpose when the enemy is hundreds of miles away, but when you hear the swords clanging, it's hard to keep everything in perspective. At such times it may be easier to think that Nebuchadnezzar, not God, is in control.

Jeremiah's prayer has gone something like this: "I know You are the Creator, the all-powerful, the loving God, the just God, the wise God, the omniscient God, the God who works in history. But frankly, God, I don't know how You are going to get Yourself out of this one."

God answers immediately and His response begins precisely where Jeremiah's prayer began: "I am the Lord, the God of all flesh. Is there anything too hard for Me?" (v. 27, KJV)

Jeremiah started with an affirmation, but ended with more questions than answers. God begins with a question and ends with positive statements. While Jeremiah began with God, he ended by dwelling on the human predicament. God begins with the human predicament, but He ends with Himself. Any time you end your time of prayer with God, there is hope.

When I was a schoolboy in junior high, my mother made a lunch for me each day to take to school. I liked peanut butter and jelly sandwiches; I hated balogna. But my mother explained that occasionally I had to have balogna and I accepted the inevitable. Once I told her, "It's OK, Mom, if you put a little bologna in the middle, as long as the two slices of bread on the outside are thick enough."

Prayer is like that, if you will pardon the crude analogy. It's OK to have some of the human predicament in the middle if you have plenty of God on both sides of it.

"Is there anything too hard for Me?" God begins.

"Not really," Jeremiah would quickly respond, if the Lord had given him time to reply. "But I still have some questions. You are holy, so I can understand punishment. But man continues to sin, so I can't understand restoration."

So God explains. After the Lord recites the sins of His people in Jeremiah 32:28-35, He tells what He is going to do. Jeremiah must have stood in awe as He heard God's amazing "I wills":

1. I will gather My people from all countries.
2. I will bring them again to this place.
3. I will cause them to dwell safely.
4. I will be their God.
5. I will give them one heart.
6. I will make an everlasting covenant with them.
7. I will put My fear in their hearts.
8. I will rejoice over them.
9. I will plant them in this land assuredly.
10. I will bring upon them all the good I have promised them.

Then just for the sake of Jeremiah, God says, "Fields will be bought again, fields that are now desolate and in the hands of the Babylonians."

Restoration is not man's doing; it is God's doing. In the New Testament we are reminded of One who "is able to do exceeding abundantly above all that we ask or think" (Eph. 3:20, KJV). So the place to start is with God's abililty. It's where Jeremiah started his prayer ("There is nothing too hard for You"); and where God began His response ("Is there anything too hard for Me?").

Often, however, the big question we ask is not "Can He?" but "Will He?" What must have been the most difficult "I will" to comprehend and a crucial one around which all the others revolved was when God said, "I will give them one heart." The heart was indeed the problem. Jeremiah had previously bemoaned its wickedness. "The heart is deceitful above all things and desperately wicked; who can know it?" (17:9, KJV)

Somehow God was going to have to do something about the heart problem. Jeremiah recognized that the covenant under which the Jews lived was an external covenant. What was needed was an internal covenant, a brand new covenant. The Old Covenant kept repeating "Thou shalt" and "Thou shalt not" and man was never able to live up to it. The New Covenant would be based on God's "I wills." Forgiveness and restoration were not enough. God's law would have to be written on the heart, not merely memorized in the head.

During his years of ministry, Jeremiah understood more and more of this concept as God revealed it to him piece by piece. But perhaps it wasn't until he was in the dungeon-prison that he put all the pieces together. Chapters 30—31 spell out in poetic form this fresh approach to man's predicament.

Maybe Jeremiah didn't have a complete New Testament understanding of it, but it is amazing what he *did* comprehend. The New Covenant, after all, is just another way of saying the New Testament. Some commentators have called Jeremiah 31:31-34 "the Gospel before the Gospel." Others have called it "certainly one of the profoundest and most moving passages in the Bible." James Leo Green calls it the "essence of Jeremiah's experience and the apex of his spiritual pilgrimage. . . . The revelation came . . . when the man who had been walking the way of a cross stood in the midst of the destruction of all that he treasured—save his relationship to God."

Somehow—and Jeremiah doesn't spell out how—the Messiah, that Righteous Branch, as he calls Him, will become our Righteousness. His law will be written in our hearts. Jeremiah also emphasizes individual responsibility. What God does in the future, the prophet says, is contingent upon individual response. The Jews of Jeremiah's day blamed their misfortunes on the sins of their forefathers, but at the same time took for granted the blessings of the covenant God had made with those same forefathers. While accepting the blessings, they denied responsibility for the evil. But Jeremiah affirms that the future relationship will be based on individual response.

At the same time, the future relationship would be based on God's irresistible grace. "I have loved you with an everlasting love," God says. "I have drawn you with loving-kindness" (31:3). In that, Jeremiah found the secret. Many of the prophets knew the holiness of God; Isaiah certainly did. Many of them knew the justice of God; Amos certainly did. Many of them knew the omnipotence of God; Daniel certainly did. But to Jeremiah was also revealed the love of God, and that was the secret piece that solved the puzzle.

In His holiness, God hates sin; in His justice, He must punish it. And if that's all we knew of God, there would be no hope for us. The Babylonians—or whoever God uses as His agents of punishment—are inevitable. The fires of hell are our destiny. There is no other solution when you consider only God's holiness and justice.

Can God do anything? Yes and no. He cannot violate His character. So even adding the omnipotence of God to the puzzle does not really solve the dilemma. Adding His omnipotence only gives you a muscle-bound God, with strength to do, but inability to perform because of His holiness and justice.

But now add the piece of the love of God, along with the omnipotence of God and you have a solution; gradually it begins to make sense. Sin has to be punished; there's no doubt about that. If God is holy and just, Jehovah Tsidkenu—the Righteous God, He must punish sin.

But in His love and omnipotence, He can take the punishment upon Himself; He can become our Righteousness. And in Jesus Christ that is exactly what happened. God's love was added to the otherwise bleak and hopeless puzzle. And adding that one piece brings life, light, and hope to the world.

Those who receive Jesus Christ not only have God's righteousness applied to their lives, but also receive a new heart on which God's laws are engraved. God's Holy Spirit becomes a permanent resident within them, and that makes what otherwise would have been an impossibility, a practical reality.

Jeremiah is still in prison; the Babylonians are still besieging the city gates. But a New Covenant is coming, a Covenant in which God will replace the old heart of stone with a heart of flesh.

Yes, there was good news for Jeremiah. Not only would his people return from exile after 70 years, but they had a glorious future ahead of them, and the New Covenant would be an everlasting Covenant.

Is there anything too hard for God?

The bars must have looked like stars to Jeremiah; the guards must have appeared like God's angels. Some prisons are made of bricks and steel, but they aren't the real prisons. The real prisons are prisons of the soul. From such a prison, Jeremiah had just been released.

How about you? Is there anything too hard for the Lord?

12

When Life Is Cheap

Jeremiah 34; 38—39

Novelist Feodor Dostoevski wrote, "If there is no God, all things are permissible." In other words, anything goes.

"How we treat people," said a businessman to theologian R.C. Sproul, "is a matter of ethics. Ethics are determined by our philosophy. Our philosophy reflects our theology. So respecting people is really a theological matter." Dostoevski and the American businessman agree.

So does Jewish philosopher Martin Buber. He put forward the idea that you may relate to what is other than yourself either by an "I-Thou" attitude or an "I-It" attitude. To oversimplify, you can treat someone as a person or as a thing.

You can also capitalize the "S" in someone, and you can treat God as a person or as a thing. God can be a vague Spirit, a great Force, or even Nature with a capital N. But it isn't until you establish an "I-Thou" relationship with God that you are truly free to establish "I-Thou" relationships with men and women.

Your relationship with God and your relationships with other people are entwined. Jesus pointed it out when He referred to the two great commandments: "Thou shalt love the Lord thy God with all thy heart, and with all thy soul, and with all thy mind," and "Thou shalt love thy neighbor as

129

thyself'' (Matt. 22:37, 39, KJV). Jeremiah knew it too.

We live in an age of narcissism, where we are instructed by paperback bestsellers to get what we can for ourselves. Life is short and we only go around once, so we must grab what we can for ourselves as soon as it comes by. We call it looking out for Number One—Numero Uno. Along with that, we have an increasing distrust of other people. Thus, life becomes increasingly empty and isolated.

On the surface, all of this seems very far removed from Jeremiah—2,600 years, 10,000 miles, and a civilization based on computer technology compared with a civilization on the verge of collapse. But it's not as far removed as you might think.

Slavery Abolished

In our last chapter, we left Jeremiah in prison. The siege of Jerusalem had resumed after a brief respite and the blockade was taking its toll on the city's morale as well as its food supply. But let's go back a few months earlier. Something took place then that ties in with the "life is cheap" motif. It occurred during the first Babylonian blockade.

King Zedekiah and the town fathers decided to free all the Jewish slaves. At first you might think that this makes Zedekiah look like Abraham Lincoln and that the action was a very noble gesture. But if you look more closely, you become a bit more suspicious about the king's motives.

Probably the first reason the city leaders decided to free the slaves was because slaves had to be fed and bread was getting more and more expensive. The second reason was that if Nebuchadnezzar stormed the walls—which he was threatening to do almost daily—slaves wouldn't fight as well as freedmen. So, militarily, it was smart to free the slaves. Third, since it was against God's Law to hold Jewish slaves, Jehovah might smile on Zedekiah if the slaves were suddenly released. Granted, Zedekiah and his cabinet hadn't been paying much attention to Jehovah lately. But in the fix that they were in, they needed all the help they could get.

A word about slavery. In some cases, slavery was permissible under the law of Moses, but only as a short-term arrangement. If a man owed you a large sum of money and was unable to pay, he could become your slave to pay it off—or until the Sabbath year—whichever came first. But such limitations had been forgotten and now slavery had become a permanent institution. Life had become cheap.

When the slaves were freed, you can imagine that Jeremiah was pleased—no matter what the motives behind it were. But his pleasure was short-lived.

You will recall that the blockade of Jerusalem was lifted to give Nebuchadnezzar time to chase the Egyptians for awhile. So when the pressure on Jerusalem was eased, Zedekiah revoked his "noble" Emancipation Proclamation. The town's leading citizens rounded up their slaves again, and life among the nobility returned to normal.

You can imagine what Jeremiah had to say about this. Thus saith the Lord: You did right in My sight when you proclaimed liberty "every man to his neighbor" (see Jer. 34:15). It's interesting that God speaks of slaves as neighbors and especially interesting in the light of how Christ says we are to love our neighbors. Jeremiah continues, perhaps with a touch of sarcasm: "But what kind of liberty did you proclaim, when you put your slaves back into servitude as soon as Nebuchadnezzar turned the other way? Therefore God will give you the same kind of liberty, and you will become slaves yourself" (see vv. 16-17).

The ancient world was full of slavery. In Rome, for instance, there were 400,000 slaves; but Jerusalem was different, at least it was supposed to be. The Children of Israel were continually reminded that they had once been slaves themselves in Egypt. Therefore, the law stipulated that Hebrew slaves be released in the sabbatical year and other slaves be released in the Year of Jubilee—the 50th year. Unlike the Roman laws by which slaves were relegated to the class of things (one ancient scholar called them "tools that speak"), the Hebrew law protected the slave. A master who put a slave to death was punished; and a slave who was ill-treated was given his freedom.

Even the patriarch Job recognized this: "If I have rejected the cause of my manservant or my maidservant when they brought a complaint against me, what then shall I do when God . . . makes inquiry?" (Job 31:13-14, RSV) The reason why masters were to treat their servants with consideration was, "God made me, and made my servant too. He created us both" (v. 15, TLB).

Human life is precious because God is the author of it. The same idea underlined Paul's teaching to the Athenians: God created from one, all the nations of the world. There is no super-race, nor super-nationality, nor super-class, nor super-sex. In the church, all this becomes a reality. Paul stressed this to the churches in Galatia: "There is neither Jew nor Greek, there is neither slave nor free man, there is neither male nor female, for you are all one in Christ Jesus" (Gal. 3:28, NASB).

Of course, this does not obliterate distinctions in society. If you go to work tomorrow morning, you will have to report to a boss. Even if he is a Christian boss, he is still a boss. But Jeremiah and Job and Paul are all saying that because bosses and employees were both created in the same divine image, they must treat each other as persons ("I-Thou" relationships), not as things ("I-It" relationships, as philosopher Martin Buber would say it).

The Cistern Experience

You can probably guess what happened next to Jeremiah. Jeremiah's words to the nobility were not received favorably, to say the least. Shortly afterward, a delegation of nobles went to King Zedekiah, demanding that Jeremiah be put to death. He had opened his mouth once too often. The king's leniency in imprisoning Jeremiah in the court of the guard rather than in a dungeon gave the prophet too much freedom. Not only was he criticizing the actions of the nobility, but he was undermining the morale of the soldiers who were guarding him. He kept advising people that the best course of action was to surrender rather than to fight. Apparently, some of the soldiers and no doubt some of the king's cabinet as well were starting to think twice about the wisdom of their present course of action. The *Revised Standard Version* says that Jeremiah was "weakening the hands of the soldiers" (38:4). In other words, he was discouraging them.

This same phrase was deciphered in a notable archeological discovery. In the 1930s, archeologists uncovered the mound that revealed the ancient city of Lachish, located about 30 miles southwest of Jerusalem. It was one of the last of the Judean cities to fall to Nebuchadnezzar, prior to the destruction of Jerusalem. As the archeologists excavated, they discovered documents written on potsherds. These documents, written in ancient Hebrew, describe Nebuchadnezzar's siege of the city. One inscription speaks of a prophet in Jerusalem. Another refers to someone "weakening the hands of the soldiers" in Jerusalem, the exact phrase used in Jeremiah 38:4. It is quite possible, though it can't be proven because Jeremiah's name isn't found on the potsherds, that the inscriptions refer to the biblical prophet. If they don't refer directly to him, they must refer to people like Baruch who had been influenced by Jeremiah.

Jeremiah's witness was felt even when he was in prison. It was something similar to Paul's experience in the Roman prison. Instead of complaining about his lot, Paul witnessed to the soldiers that were guarding him and many of them became Christians.

Like Paul and like Jeremiah, you may feel imprisoned. Health, family problems, age, or other circumstances may entrap you. Your witness appears extremely limited, and you wish for more opportunities.

But God calls us to be faithful where we are, even in the darkest of circumstances. There may be soldiers, whom we look upon as our captors, who are themselves enslaved, and who need the freedom that only the Lord can provide.

Who else would have been able to witness to the Roman soldiers if Paul hadn't? Who else would have been able to witness to the Hebrew soldiers if Jeremiah hadn't? The opportunities for such witnessing may be part of the reason why God allows the imprisonment.

Irate because Jeremiah was speaking out even when he was in prison, the city fathers went to the king. "Jeremiah must die," they demanded. In typical fashion, King Zedekiah responded, "Very well, he is in your hands; the king can do nothing to stop you" (see 38:5). Zedekiah was doing the Pontius Pilate act. He was washing his hands of Jeremiah's future; he was concerned only about his own. Ironically, he would have had a future if he had followed the advice of Jeremiah instead of following the advice of his nobles.

Popularity continued to be important to Zedekiah. People could be sacrificed, but he must look after his own interests. Having been placed on the throne by Nebuchadnezzar, succeeding the popular young King Jehoiachin, Zedekiah found it difficult to win any popularity contests in Jerusalem. So he tried to get a place in his people's hearts by appeasing them and going whatever way the wind blew.

Instead of sending Jeremiah to a quick death, the nobles decided that slow death would be the best way to handle the pesky prophet. So they sent him back to solitary confinement. A few months earlier he had been confined in a subterranean dungeon (chap. 37); now he was placed in a miry cistern. It was the harshest punishment he had faced thus far.

His accusers did not want to bear the onus of slaying someone who might be a true prophet of Jehovah. But their consciences wouldn't disturb them if they threw him into a cistern and let nature take its course. (It reminds me of Joseph's brothers in Genesis 37.)

A cistern of that day was usually pear-shaped, cut out of limestone rock. At its neck, the cistern would probably be only three feet across, but down below it opened up into a larger bulbous cavity. Even in the dry seasons, water would seep into the cisterns from various sources and the floor of the cistern would be muddy at best; often several inches of mud would line the bottom. The Bible says simply that Jeremiah "sank down into the mud"(38:6). That describes the physical scene, but emotional and psychological effects on Jeremiah are better reflected in another passage of Scripture.

Many Bible scholars feel that Psalm 69 was composed by Jeremiah during the time that he was in his cistern prison. The inscription of the psalm says "a psalm of David," but these inscriptions were added later by Jewish rabbis and lay no claim to divine inspiration. Because the psalm resembles Lamentations 3, because it speaks about the future rebuilding of Judah as if Jerusalem's destruction were imminent, and because it seems to describe Jeremiah's cistern confinement so graphically, many scholars think Jeremiah may have been its author.

It certainly doesn't take much imagination to think of Jeremiah saying, in the words of the psalm, "I have sunk into the mire of the deep where there is no foothold. . . . I am worn out with my crying; my throat is hoarse; my eyes failed as I cried for my God. . . . I have become estranged from my brethren, an alien from my mother's sons. . . . When I made sackcloth my garment, then I became a byword to them. . . . Rescue me out of the mire, lest I sink. . . . Let not the pit shut its mouth over me. . . . I hoped for sympathy and there was none, and for comforters but I found none. . . . The Lord hears the poor, and He has never ignored His prisoners" (H.C. Leopold, *Exposition of the Psalms,* Baker).

G. Campbell Morgan writes, "Perhaps in no psalm in the whole psalter is the sense of sorrow profounder or more intense than in this."

For Jeremiah, it always seemed that he would go one step forward and two steps back. The Lord would deliver him from one calamity and before long Jeremiah would find himself in even a more perplexing situation. And so once again we find Jeremiah earnestly praying for deliverance.

An Unlikely Hero
But while Jeremiah was fervently beseeching God from his underground chamber, God was preparing a deliverer above

ground. Of course, Jeremiah had no idea what was going on aboveground. In fact, he must have thought that God was taking a long time to answer his prayer. But God was working in Jeremiah's behalf all the time. It is typical of the Lord to be doing things above us of which we are totally unaware. We seldom know whom the Lord is preparing to be our deliverer, our comforter, our encourager, or whatever we may need. Often it is a very unlikely person.

Jeremiah's deliverer was both an unusual person and in an unusual position. He was a black-skinned man, an Ethiopian. Jeremiah had once asked the rhetorical question, "Can the Ethiopian change his skin?" (13:23) There weren't too many Ethiopians walking around Jerusalem in Jeremiah's day, and it may have been that his future deliverer was the one that he was referring to when he asked the question.

The name that the Bible gives to him is Ebed-Melech, but the literal meaning of the name is "slave of the king." So it is quite possible that Ebed-Melech is more a descriptive title than an official name. Though he was an Ethiopian slave, he held a trusted position in Zedekiah's palace. Through the years he had undoubtedly observed Jeremiah's comings and goings. He had also witnessed the connivings of the king's cabinet and the vacillations of his master the king.

Ebed-Melech had seen what had happened to Jeremiah after he had denounced the nobles for bringing their slaves back into captivity, and he had seen how the nobles had thrown Jeremiah into a cistern where he would be facing certain death. As a trusted servant in the king's palace, Ebed-Melech observed a great deal, but said little. That was his job. In fact, he probably knew more about what was going on in Jerusalem than King Zedekiah did himself. And, of course, there were always some things that the king preferred not to know, such as what the nobles really did with Jeremiah.

Ebed-Melech decided to take some action on the Jeremiah matter on a day that the king was hearing complaints in the Benjamin Gate. Even though Nebuchadnezzar was storming the walls, King Zedekiah was still trying to win friends and influence his constituency. He had learned the trick from Absalom who, years before, had done the same thing in an attempt to win popular support at the expense of his father David (2 Sam. 15:2-6).

No doubt, Zedekiah was a bit surprised to see his own slave Ebed-Melech approach him with a complaint. After all, Ebed-Melech wasn't even a Jew, and besides, if he had a problem, he could talk to the king about it in the palace rather than in public where others would hear him.

But Ebed-Melech knew what he was doing. It wasn't unusual for prisoners to be thrust into cisterns, but it *was* unusual for such prisoners to come out alive. Archeologists have unearthed a cistern in Gezer that contained 12 skeletons, perhaps of prisoners like Jeremiah.

It was dangerous for Ebed-Melech to make a public case of it, but it would insure action. With people all around, some of whom might be somewhat sympathetic to Jeremiah, Zedekiah would have to do something. So Ebed-Melech bravely stated his case. "Jeremiah is as good as dead if you let him stay in the cistern," he said (Jer. 38:9).

"Well then, get him out," replied the king, as if he had nothing to do with Jeremiah being there in the first place.

Ebed-Melech wasted no time. He recruited his helpers, got some old rags and clothes from a storeroom and then went to the cistern to hoist out the prophet. Why the old rags and clothes? The Ethiopian slave knew that if he tried to lift Jeremiah out with ropes, they would cut into the flesh of the starving prophet. So considerately he got rags and clothing to prevent Jeremiah from being hurt in the rescue operation.

There's a lesson here for us. Not only *what* we do, but also *how* we do it is important. Whether it is witnessing or showing mercy, we sometimes do it as if we were obeying a command, but hating every moment of it. In Romans 12, as Paul delineates some of the spiritual gifts, he emphasizes the importance of the *how* as well as the *what*. Even those who show mercy are reminded that it is to be done with cheerfulness. In other words, Christian service must be done with an "I-Thou" attitude, not with an "I-It" attitude. Ebed-Melech was not merely thinking of rescue; he was thinking of Jeremiah. Similarly, in witnessing, we must not merely be interested in saving souls; we must be interested in people.

We don't know for certain why Ebed-Melech put his life on the line for Jeremiah, but we can make some guesses. First, he may have appreciated Jeremiah's blast at the king and the nobles for their flip-flop on the edict to free the slaves. Though the edict involved only Hebrew slaves, Ebed-Melech would certainly have been sympathetic to their plight.

Second, Ebed-Melech trusted in the Lord. A Gentile, he had come to Jerusalem and had put his faith in Jehovah. How do we know this? Well, like Baruch, Ebed-Melech is given his own section of Scripture.

Seldom is a Gentile addressed personally in a section of Scripture, and Ebed-Melech was not only a Gentile, but a servant as well. Nevertheless Jeremiah 39:15-18 is addressed personally to a black man named Ebed-Melech. In this passage God promises Ebed-Melech deliverance during the difficult days that were ahead. "I will surely keep you safe . . . because you trusted in Me." (Jer. 39:18, from *The Book of Jeremiah* translated by J.A. Thompson, Eerdmans).

King Zedekiah did everything he could to please the people and save his own neck. His servant, Ebed-Melech, risked his position and maybe even his own life to rescue Jeremiah. In the end, it was Ebed-Melech who was delivered from the enemy—not Zedekiah.

Cheapening Life

Poor Zedekiah. Nothing he did worked out as he had hoped. He thought that by putting Jeremiah in the hands of his nobles, he would appease the nobles and not have to worry about Jeremiah any more. Then Ebed-Melech interfered, and Zedekiah had to permit Jeremiah's release. Now he would be in trouble with his nobles again.

If only he could get some concessions from Jeremiah. If only Jeremiah would adjust his message a little bit. So Zedekiah asked for another private meeting with the prophet. It was at the king's royal entrance to the temple, a spot where the nobles were certain not to see them talking together.

The king was hoping that Jeremiah would be grateful that he had given the order to Ebed-Melech to rescue him. If he hadn't given that order, Jeremiah would still be languishing at the bottom of the cistern. Maybe Jeremiah would even be grateful enough to soften his message.

Now imagine yourself to be Jeremiah. You have just been rescued from slow death by Ebed-Melech, acting with the king's approval. You are summoned once again before the king. Once again, he asks you for the Word of the Lord.

Aren't you tempted to change your tune? For nearly 40 years you've been preaching the same line and what has it gotten you? Persecution and more persecution. Nobody listens; nobody repents—and God doesn't even give you any pats on the back. Why not change the message now and enjoy life a little? But Jeremiah didn't change his tune. His commitment to God's truth was as steadfast as ever.

After his meeting with King Zedekiah, Jeremiah was returned to the court of the guard, which must have seemed like a luxury prison when compared with the cistern. There Jeremiah stayed until Jerusalem fell to the Babylonians.

It was July 587 B.C. when the city fell. The siege had begun 18 months earlier, and except for a couple months during the summer of 588, the people of the city had been facing increasing hardships. During the final months, hunger grew more severe; many people were starving.

Jeremiah 52 tells the story of the city's destruction: "The famine in the city had become so severe that there was no food for the people to eat. Then the city wall was broken through, and the whole army fled" (vv. 6-7). F.B. Meyer paints the gruesome picture: "Imagine for a moment the overcrowded city, into which had gathered from all the country round, the peasantry and villagers, who, with such of their valuables as they had been able hastily to collect and transport, had sought refuge within the gray old walls of Zion from the violence and outrage of merciless troops."

Garbage and refuse accumulated on the city streets. Barley cakes were mingled with cow's dung to stretch the dwindling food supply. Young children cried for bread, but got none. Then the famine was exacerbated by plague. Bodies of the dying and the dead lay in the streets and no one had the time, the place, or the inclination to bury them. The stench became unbearable.

You can imagine Jeremiah as he emerged from the court of the guard. He had been imprisoned for about a year—in a dungeon, in a courtyard, in a cistern, and then back in the courtyard of the guard again. He had heard of how the people were suffering because of Zedekiah's inflexibility. No doubt friends like Baruch relayed as best they could the grim facts. But until Jeremiah stepped outside his prison, he could not possibly have imagined how devastating the siege had been.

The Book of Lamentations was written as Jeremiah surveyed the streets of the city shortly after the invading army stormed through. "Is it nothing to you, all you who pass by?" he asks (1:12). But in Lamentations 4 the prophet depicts man's inhumanity to man: "The tongue of the infant clings to the roof of its mouth for thirst; the young children ask for bread, but no one breaks it for them. Those who ate delicacies are desolate in the streets. . . . Their skin clings to their bones. . . . The hands of the compassionate women have cooked their own children" (vv. 4-5, 8, 10, NKJV).

Life had been cheap in Jerusalem, and it was getting cheaper. Babies had been sacrificed on the altars of Molech outside the city; slaves had been kept, contrary to the law; and then in times of extreme crisis, mothers had eaten their own babies.

Life is cheap in our day as well, and it is getting cheaper. Our children grow up using toy guns, pretending that they are killing their playmates; they fill their leisure hours by watching TV characters live by violence and mayhem. In our society, abortion has become commonplace and homicides are so prevalent that they can't make the evening news; even in sports it takes violence or the probability of a serious accident to attract the fans.

But there are other ways that we cheapen life, ways that seem more innocent than abortion and euthanasia. We cheapen life when we "use" people to accomplish our purposes. It seems natural to us to do so. Everything we touch becomes a consumer product, including people. If we can't use them, they can be discarded. And even if we *can* use them, they are discarded as soon as their value to us is finished. Unfortunately, even churches have a tendency to do this. Church members are sometimes seen in terms of what they can do for the church. When they are not deemed useful, they are discarded like a used Kleenex.

Zedekiah was a people-user. He used Jeremiah, or rather he *tried* to use him—but he was never successful. He saw people as useful if they could benefit him. Basically he was not a mean man; he was selfish. Zedekiah didn't even realize where Jeremiah had been imprisoned. He had erased Jeremiah from his memory until Ebed-Melech intruded.

On the other hand, Ebed-Melech was people-sensitive. As a servant, he had been trained to be aware of needs before they were even voiced; that is the way every Christian should be trained. People were important to Ebed-Melech; life was valuable. It hurt him when life was cheapened.

"Life," wrote William Shakespeare in *Macbeth,* "is a tale told by an idiot, full of sound and fury, signifying nothing." But that's not the biblical attitude. The Bible says that life is precious and has infinite meaning. It is a gift of God, and no one should disparage a gift that God has given.

13

When You Don't Feel Like Getting Out of Bed in the Morning

Jeremiah 40—44; 50—51; Lamentations

Some mornings you don't want to get up. You know what is out there and you don't think you can face it.

Jeremiah must have felt like that. He was about 60 years old now. For about 40 years he had been preaching, and his basic theme had been, "Repent or Jerusalem will be destroyed by the Babylonians." The people hadn't repented, and the city had been demolished.

Chaos and Anarchy

What was there left for Jeremiah to look forward to? His marching orders from God had concluded with the destruction of Jerusalem. And at 60 you don't look forward to starting a new job. If ever there was a good time to quit the prophet business, this was it.

Dr. James M. Boice of the "Bible Study Hour" radio broadcast speaks of Jeremiah as having a commitment to people above programs, a commitment to place above promotion, and a commitment to permanence. It's true. Jeremiah loved his people, he loved Jerusalem, and he faithfully preached for nearly 40 years in the same place with virtually nothing to show for it.

Yes, Jeremiah was committed to people. But he saw the

142

people he loved fleeing in horror from the vicious Babylonian armies. For 18 months those soldiers had been frustrated outside the walls of the city. They were not accustomed to waiting for military victory. Each month that Jerusalem held out, the rage of the soldiers was growing. Now they were unleashing all that pent-up furor and savagery upon men, women, and children. Jeremiah saw the bodies of people he loved littering the narrow city streets.

As for his commitment to place, his city of Jerusalem was now a shambles. Its cherished buildings were strewn brick by brick. And permanence? The word had lost its meaning.

But even in such times of desolation, God can be honored by our faithfulness. Even in times when we are in a state of shock, numbed by trauma, stumbling, reeling, hardly knowing what we are doing, God will take our hands and lead us.

Sometime during this period, Jeremiah wrote the following words: "He has besieged me and surrounded me with bitterness and hardship. He has made me dwell in darkness like those long dead. . . . I have been deprived of peace. I have forgotten what prosperity is. . . . Yet this I call to mind and therefore I have hope. . . . I say to myself, 'The Lord is my portion; therefore I will wait for Him.' . . . It is good to wait quietly for the salvation of the Lord" (Lam. 3:5-6, 17, 21, 24, 26).

Earlier in his life Jeremiah was impatient with the Lord. But he had learned. And now, though he had ministered faithfully for 40 years, he was still content to wait.

He knew that God was there, and he knew that even in the chaos God had something in mind for him.

"They tried to end my life in a pit," he recalled, "and threw stones at me; the waters closed over my head, and I thought I was about to be cut off. I called on Your name, O Lord, from the depths of the pit. You heard my plea: 'Do not close Your ears to my cry for relief.' You came near when I called You, and You said, 'Do not fear.' O Lord, You took up my case; You redeemed my life" (Lam. 3:53-58).

Chaos and anarchy reigned in the place of King Zedekiah. If

ever Jeremiah needed to hear God say, "Do not fear," it was now.

And what happened to King Zedekiah? The events of those days after the Babylonians stormed into Jerusalem in July 587 B.C. can be pieced together from five different passages of Scripture (Jer. 39—40; 52; 2 Kings 25; 2 Chron. 36).

When King Zedekiah saw the Babylonian soldiers storming into the city, he hid until evening and then escaped in the darkness. It was probably via a secret exit, through his royal garden near the Pool of Siloam. He followed the Jericho Road across the Judean Wilderness down into the Jordan Valley. He thought that once he got to the Jordan Valley he could elude the soldiers. Jeremiah had once spoken about the jungle growth of the Jordan Valley (Jer. 12:5). Wild animals made it dangerous, but Zedekiah was willing to take the risk rather than fall into the hands of Nebuchadnezzar.

Shortly before Zedekiah could get to Jericho, however, he was captured by the Babylonians. In chains he was taken 150 miles north to Riblah for a military trial. There Nebuchadnezzar declared Zedekiah and his sons guilty of treason. Zedekiah watched as his sons were executed. It was the last thing that Zedekiah ever saw. Immediately after the executions, Zedekiah's eyes were poked out. Then, still in chains, Zedekiah was taken by soldiers to Babylon (52:7-11). There he lived as a grim example to other puppet governors who might decide to launch uprisings against their Babylonian overlords.

Jeremiah had prophesied that Zedekiah would see Nebuchadnezzar and then be taken to Babylon (34:2-3). Ezekiel had prophesied that Zedekiah would die in Babylon without ever seeing it (Ezek. 12:10-13). Both prophecies were fulfilled.

Off to Ramah

What happened to Jeremiah? The Chaldean leaders, including Nebuchadnezzar himself, were aware of what Jeremiah had prophesied. In fact, they knew he was in prison during their lengthy siege. So when the city was invaded, word was passed along to the invading troops to release Jeremiah.

Scripture doesn't say exactly what happened next, but apparently after his release, Jeremiah went out to find Baruch and Ebed-Melech, both of whom had befriended him when he was in trouble. As Jeremiah edged his way through the distraught throngs milling through the Jerusalem streets, he was seized by other Babylonian soldiers.

Before long, he found himself in chains, herded no doubt with Baruch and Ebed-Melech and hundreds, maybe thousands of others, to Ramah, about five miles north of Jerusalem. Ramah was the military camp where Nebuchadnezzar's commander Nebuzaradan had set up his headquarters. (Literally, Nebuzaradan's title was "chief of the butchers.")

The Babylonians' strategy was to deport the rich, the wise, and the mighty, and bring them back to Babylon. There they could be rehabilitated, brainwashed, and kept watch on. They left poor peasant farmers in the country to tend the fields. Nebuchadnezzar felt there was no advantage in allowing the land to lie fallow.

Jeremiah knew all this, of course. There had already been two previous deportations. One took place in 605 or 606 B.C. when a few promising young men like Daniel were taken to Babylon. Less than a decade later Nebuchadnezzar came in force, removing Jehoiachin from his throne and deporting him along with about 10,000 others, including the Prophet Ezekiel. Of this number, perhaps 3,000 were adult males; the rest were women and children. (See Jer. 52:28.)

Now another decade had passed. Disease, famine, and the 18-month siege had decimated the city, and it must have been a sorry lot that trudged those miles to Ramah. King Zedekiah, his sons, and his nobles had already been captured and judged. Only the common folk were left.

At Ramah, Jeremiah was brought face to face with Nebuzaradan, chief of the butchers. When Jeremiah identified himself by name, Nebuzaradan realized that a mistake had been made and gave a remarkable confession to the prophet. In fact, Nebuzaradan almost sounded like a prophet himself. It was Jehovah who had caused the destruction of Jerusalem, the heathen general said, "because you sinned against the Lord and did not obey His voice (40:3, RSV). As remarkable as the statement is, it probably does not indicate the general's faith as much as his knowledge of Jeremiah's prophecies.

In appreciation of Jeremiah's prophetic utterances that had urged the people to surrender to Babylon, the general gave the aging prophet two choices: (1) to return to Babylon and spend his retirement years in ease and honor, or (2) to stay in Palestine in the rubble and unrest that characterized the defeated land. If Jeremiah went to Babylon, Nebuzaradan himself would look after him; if he stayed in Palestine, the newly appointed governor of the land, Gedaliah, would watch over him. (The fact that someone was designated to watch over him may indicate that Jeremiah's health had been severely impaired in his recent imprisonment.)

Well, Jeremiah, what about quitting now?

Earlier in his ministry, Jeremiah had wanted to run away from it all. "O that I had in the desert a wayfarers' lodging place, that I might leave my people and go away from them!" (9:2, RSV) Now he had the opportunity.

The Captive Prophet

But he didn't take it. Jeremiah chose to stay in Palestine. The Jewish historian Josephus says that Jeremiah told the general that "he would gladly live in the ruins of the country and in the miserable remains of it."

Sensing that, Nebuzaradan gave him ample supplies and sent him nearby to Mizpah, where the new governor was setting up his administration. (Jerusalem had been so utterly demolished that it was not a fit place for any government.)

Gedaliah, the new governor, was a good man. His grandfather Shaphan had served as King Josiah's secretary and had carried the newly discovered scroll of the Law to the king. Gedaliah's father had offered protection to Jeremiah when the prophet was almost lynched outside the temple. So Jeremiah was no doubt pleased with the choice of Gedaliah as governor. Indeed some scholars feel that Jeremiah may have been instrumental in suggesting Gedaliah for the job.

Gedaliah was not called king, but governor. Nebuchadnez-zar had enough of kings whose titles were larger than their brains. Moreover, Gedaliah was not of the royal line. But if he did a good job as governor he might be permitted to marry one of the daughters of the royal line and eventually be allowed to wear the crown. That was probably the carrot that Nebuchadnezzar dangled in front of Gedaliah.

Gedaliah ruled well. He brought dissident factions together. Some of the Jews had fled to neighboring lands; slowly they returned. Others had been hiding in caves; still others had fled to the hills or to the Jordan Valley and were waging sporadic guerrilla attacks on the Babylonian forces. Gedaliah succeed-ed in pacifying them.

In fact, things were going so well that Gedaliah got the notion that he had no enemies. His biggest problem may have been that he was naive. When he was told that Ishmael, a guerrilla commander and a member of the royal house, was plotting to assassinate him, he couldn't believe it. Undoubted-ly, he knew Ishmael, but apparently he didn't know him well enough.

One day Gedaliah invited Ishmael to dinner in the gover-nor's house (perhaps to demonstrate his trust of Ishmael). It was an opportunity that Ishmael couldn't pass up. Before the infamous evening had ended, Ishmael had slain Gedaliah in cold blood, and Ishmael's trained guerrillas murdered Geda-liah's aides and his Chaldean bodyguards (41:1-3).

But Ishmael wasn't finished yet. Ishmael wanted to take away with him as much food and weaponry as he could. So while some of his men terrorized the local citizenry, the others gathered supplies. Included in the terrorized local citizenry were both Jeremiah and Baruch as well as several princesses and a few other soldiers and townspeople. Ishmael had no qualms about killing governors, but he didn't relish killing prophets or princesses.

It seems that Ishmael had no qualms about killing pilgrims either. A day later, 80 pilgrims were on their way from the north to worship on the ruins of the Jerusalem temple. At Mizpah they halted to pay their respects to the new governor Gedaliah, not knowing of the massacre. Ishmael lured them inside, killed 70 of them and dumped their bodies into a cistern. Ten of the pilgrims saved their lives by telling Ishmael where he could find more food (vv. 4-8).

Now Ishmael realized he could waste no more time. He grabbed his captives—Jeremiah, Baruch, the princesses, and the others—along with his loot and hurried in the direction of Ammon, whose king was Ishmael's ally and a co-conspirator in the assassination of Gedaliah.

Once again Jeremiah was in serious trouble. The year was probably 583 B.C. (some scholars say 586 B.C.) and Jeremiah was getting close to 65 years old. A forced march with a bloody assassin was hardly what the aging prophet needed.

Fortunately, before Ishmael and his captives got too far, Johanan, a military leader loyal to Gedaliah, caught up with them. Another battle; more bloodshed. Ishmael and eight of his men escaped to Ammon, but Jeremiah and the other captives were rescued (vv. 11-15).

Now Johanan was in charge, and frankly he didn't know what to do. As soon as Nebuchadnezzar found out that not only had Gedaliah been slain, but also several Babylonian soldiers, there would be reprisals. More bloodshed. And Johanan feared that it would be his own blood.

His first reaction was to flee to Egypt. He gathered his band—which of course included Jeremiah and Baruch and perhaps as many as a hundred others—and they made their way southward. But there was some uncertainty among the band regarding their course of action. When they stopped at a caravansary south of Jerusalem in Bethlehem, they talked it over. Still undecided, the people all came to Jeremiah to ask him to pray to God for divine direction (41:16—42:3).

They did not seek Jeremiah's human wisdom or even his wisdom accumulated from 40 years as a prophet. What they wanted was the Word of the Lord. Jeremiah was just as interested in knowing the Lord's will as the people were. So he prayed and waited for the Lord's answer.

We Know What We Want

All of this sounds good; the problem was that while the petitioners felt they needed to inquire of the Lord regarding such a major move as this, they knew in advance the answer they wanted. They wanted a "go" sign, not a "stop" sign.

It is certainly difficult to pray without strong feelings about the answer we desire. But when the answer is received, we should be willing to obey it, whether or not it satisfies us. These people not only unanimously asked Jeremiah to pray, but they also unanimously promised to obey everything the Lord would tell Jeremiah.

Day by day the people waited—no doubt with growing impatience—for an answer from the Lord. And every day that they waited was another day that Nebuchadnezzar might find them and put them to death for what had happened in Mizpah. So every day that they waited, they became more anxious to get on the road to Egypt.

Surely it was difficult for Jeremiah to wait as well. His life was also in jeopardy. He knew how much the people wanted an immediate answer. But he waited and waited until he had God's response.

After 10 days the response finally came, but it wasn't the response that the people wanted.

One commentator opines that Jeremiah's time at Mizpah "may have been the easiest, happiest time of his ministry. For a short season he was free from the burden of proclaiming judgment and was at liberty to set forth the glowing prospect and glorious promises regarding the future of God's people."

But now at Bethlehem, things had returned to normal. Jeremiah was presenting words that the people did not want to hear. "Remain in the land, and God will take care of you. If you go to Egypt, you will suffer from war, famine, and disease. Do not go to Egypt" (see 42:9-22).

The people couldn't receive the message. After 10 days of waiting, they felt more than ever that they had to go to Egypt.

"You're lying," they told Jeremiah. "God did not give you that message; Baruch did" (43:1-3). Perhaps because of Jeremiah's age and health, the people thought that he might be getting his counsel from a younger man, Baruch, instead of from the Lord. But age is no barrier for God's message.

Of course, Jeremiah's personal preference was to stay in his homeland and live his remaining days there. Because it suited him, he could have given such a message on the first day. For years, he had been decrying the tendency to resort to Egypt for help, and he could have pulled an old sermon from his bag and preached it to the people on the first day. But he didn't. He wanted God's will, not his own, for the people.

No matter what words came from the prophet's mouth, Johanan's mind had already been made up, and most of the people agreed with him. They must head south, as quickly as possible, toward Egypt. Jeremiah and Baruch had no choice. They were forced to accompany the others. To Jeremiah, it seemed to be a tragic conclusion to a life-long struggle.

Jeremiah knew that whenever the Israelites ventured to Egypt—whether it was Abraham, Isaac, Joseph, or whoever—they were asking for trouble.

Of course, not all of the Jews were returning to Egypt with Johanan's company. Some peasants were still residing in Palestine; thousands of others were captive in Babylon. But Jeremiah was sure that the group in which he was included was going into Egypt against the will of the Lord. In Egypt, Johanan's band apparently joined other Jews who had previously emigrated there.

The fact that Jeremiah was an unwilling resident in Egypt did not prevent him from proclaiming God's message. Basically, he had a two-point sermon. First of all, he kept pointing out that there was no safety in Egypt. Safety is not found in places; it is found in God's presence.

To emphasize the point, he buried some large stones in pavement in front of a government residence. Then he declared that Nebuchadnezzar would come and put up his throne on those buried stones (43:9-13). According to Jeremiah's colorful language, Nebuchadnezzar would "pick the land of Egypt clean as a shepherd picks lice from his clothing" (from *The Book of Jeremiah* translated by J.A. Thompson, Eerdmans). Fifteen years later, Nebuchadnezzar did indeed invade Egypt even as Jeremiah had predicted.

Second, Jeremiah warned that idolatry in Egypt was no better than idolatry in Jerusalem. The prophet couldn't understand how anyone who had seen the judgment of God upon Jerusalem because of apostasy could think of worshiping idols in Egypt.

Even more astonishing was the people's reply. They responded that during the times of the worst idolatry in Israel, there was relative peace and tranquility. It was only after the revival of King Josiah's time that Babylon had risen up to give them trouble. To Jeremiah, it must have been unbelievable. "We will continue to burn sacrifices to the Queen of Heaven," they said stubbornly (see 44:15-17).

"Go ahead," Jeremiah responded, "and you will see what happens." The result, he said, would be the virtual annihilation of all the Jewish refugees in Egypt. With those ominous words, the spoken ministry of Jeremiah concluded. The year was probably 579 or 580 B.C. The prophet was between 65 and 70 years old. He had been preaching for about 45 years— with very few visible results. Even in Egypt the people didn't listen.

Jeremiah's Last Prophecy

There's another side to the assessment of Jeremiah's ministry. Commentator J.A. Thompson writes, "It has often been remarked that Jeremiah's life was finally a failure. He was alone for most of his ministry. It seemed that no one gave any heed to his words. He was dragged off finally to live his last days in exile against his own will. He was a failure as the world judges human achievement. But a more balanced assessment of him would be that his very words of judgment saved Israel's faith from disintegration and his words of hope finally helped his people to gain hope in God's future for them."

While Jeremiah's oral ministry may have concluded with his judgment on the Jewish refugees in Egypt in Jeremiah 44, the last words of his written ministry may have been his judgment on Babylon in chapters 50—51.

E.J. Young feels that Jeremiah had completed a first draft of his book in 594 B.C. and later—probably when he was in Egypt—he expanded it to its present length.

Along with his prophecy of judgment for Babylon, Jeremiah gives hope for the Jews in exile there. Looking into the future, Jeremiah predicts: "In those days, and in that time, saith the Lord, the Children of Israel shall come, they and the Children of Judah together, going and weeping; they shall go, and seek the Lord their God. They shall ask the way to Zion with their faces thitherward, saying, 'Come, and let us join ourselves to the Lord in a perpetual covenant that shall not be forgotten' "(50:4-5, KJV).

When he wrote those words, it may have been 50 years since God had called him into the prophetic ministry. And while there had been much gloom and doom in his message, you could always find a glimmer of hope, if you looked hard enough. Jeremiah saw the day coming when the Jewish exiles would return. They would be weeping as they came back. Their repentance would be accompanied by affirmative action. But tears do not speak only of sorrow; often they speak of joy. And what is more joyful and more tearful than a homecoming?

Jeremiah could look beyond exile in Babylon and his own forced flight to Egypt and see a glorious homecoming ahead. Along with the weeping and going was a seeking and a committing on the part of the returning Jews. They were on their way back to God. They weren't proud of where they had been, but they knew where they were going and they wouldn't rest until they got there.

Philip Henry, father of the famous Bible commentator Matthew Henry, was engaged to a young woman whose parents opposed the marriage. "We do not know where he has come from," they told their daughter. She responded, "You may not know where he has come from, but I know where he is going to, and I want to go along with him."

Jeremiah is often described only as a prophet of doom and destruction. But he became a prophet of hope. Jeremiah's initial call from God (1:10) designated him to pluck up, to break down, to destroy, and to overthrow—all negative. But he was also to build and to plant. The more he got to know his God, the more he understood God's greatness. And when you understand God's greatness, there is hope.

Jeremiah was also keenly aware that Jehovah was not a local deity. His people might be exiled to Babylon or Egypt, but God was still there. Jeremiah lived with the personal awareness of God's presence day by day.

The *New Bible Dictionary* says that though the emotional, highly strung prophet had "fierce internal conflicts" early in his ministry, he found in God a refuge. "Thus, the Old Testament ideal of communion with God comes to its finest expression in Jeremiah." And it was in this fellowship with God that Jeremiah was able finally to withstand the erosive effects of timidity, anguish, helplessness, hostility, loneliness, despair, misunderstanding, and failure. Can a close walk with God do all that for you? It surely can.

Sir John Franklin was an early explorer of the Arctic. For a quarter of a century during the early 1800s, he probed the desolate and barren North Pole area. He was the discoverer of the Northwest Passage, but he himself eventually became a victim of that frigid region. Explorers found his body 10 years later.

In one of his frozen books was a page with a leaf turned to mark the passage. A Bible verse was pointed out: "Fear not. . . . When thou passest through the waters, I will be with thee, and through the rivers, they shall not overflow thee" (Isa. 43:1-2, KJV). Like Jeremiah, explorer John Franklin faced a lonely life, a life in which he was often tempted to give up. But he never surrendered to that temptation. He refused to quit, and he had the courage to go anywhere because he had the confidence of God's presence.

Alfred Lord Tennyson memorialized him in a monument in London's Westminster Abbey:

> Not here! The White North hath thy bones, and
>   thou
> Heroic Sailor Soul!
> Art passing on thy happier voyage now
>   Towards no earthly Pole.

Another poem by Tennyson, "Enoch Arden," tells the story of another lost seaman. As he leaves his home and wife, he says:

> Keep everything shipshape, for I must go!
> And fear no more for me, or if you fear,
> Cast all your cares on God; that anchor holds!
> Is He not yonder in those uttermost
> Parts of the morning? If I flee to these,
> Can I go from Him? And the sea is His;
> The sea is His; He made it.

That is the God that Jeremiah knew and in whose presence Jeremiah lived.

Scripture doesn't record the death of Jeremiah. Early Christian tradition says he was stoned to death in Egypt. Jewish rabbis say that when Nebuchadnezzar invaded Egypt in 568 B.C., he took Jeremiah and Baruch back with him to Babylon. There is even a story that Jeremiah and Baruch were able to leave Egypt on their own and return to the land of Judah. No one knows. It doesn't matter.

What matters is that Jeremiah was God's man until his death. He never quit.

Bibliography

Campbell, Frank R. *God's Message in Troubled Times.* Nashville, Tenn.: Broadman Press, 1981.

Erdman, Charles R. *The Book of Jeremiah.* Westwood, N.J.: Fleming H. Revell Company, 1955.

Feinberg, Charles L. *Jeremiah: A Commentary.* Grand Rapids, Mich.: Zondervan Publishing House, 1982.

Harrison, R.K. *Jeremiah and Lamentations.* Downers Grove, Ill.: InterVarsity Press, 1973.

Howard, David M. *Words of Fire; Rivers of Tears: The Man Jeremiah.* Wheaton, Ill.: Tyndale House Publishers, 1976.

Huey, F.B., Jr. *Jeremiah: A Study Guide Commentary.* Grand Rapids, Mich.: Zondervan Publishing House, 1981.

Ironside, H.A. *Jeremiah: Prophecy and Lamentations.* Neptune, N.J.: Loizeaux Brothers, 1906.

LaSor, William Sanford. *Great Personalities of the Bible.* Westwood, N.J.: Fleming H. Revell Company, 1965.

Meyer, F.B. *Jeremiah.* Fort Washington, Pa.: Christian Literature Crusade, 1980.

Smith, George Adam. *Jeremiah.* London, England: Hodder and Stoughton, 1923.

Stewart, Alexander. *Jeremiah.* Edinburgh, Scotland: Knox Press, 1936.

Thompson, J.A. *The Book of Jeremiah.* Grand Rapids, Mich.: William B. Eerdmans Publishing Company, 1980.

White, K. Owen. *The Book of Jeremiah.* Grand Rapids, Mich.: Baker Book House, 1961.